Medium Well

The Journey from Believing to Believing In

Donn King

Hidden Mentor Media

The story and characters in this business fable are fictitious. Certain real-life locations are recognizable. The story is based on the real-life circumstances of the author and his family. It is not, however, autobiographical. Many of the specific details are completely fictitious. Do not assume anything you read here is factual.

Book Cover by 100 Covers

First edition 2024

ISBN (ebook): 979-8-9893121-3-9
ISBN (paperback): 979-8-9893121-4-6
ISBN (hardcover): 979-8-9893121-5-3

Published by
Hidden Mentor Media
257 N. Calderwood St. #327
Alcoa, TN 37701

DonnKing.com

Contents

This book is dedicated to all those hospital workers, from doctors to nurses to technicians to cleaning staff to administrators who have worked together to keep children like our daughter alive, and living the best life they can. You are true heroes.

And also to the people working in various sorts of bureaucracies who labored to find ways to bend a broken system in service of real people. Ask me sometime about the insurance case manager who risked her job to make sure our daughter didn't die choking on red tape.

Praise

"*Medium Well* is a touching parable of a young woman who learns that she possesses a special ability that isn't widely accepted. Through the support of mentors who show her the beauty of believing in yourself—even when you're different, we watch her encourage others to have open minds and hearts, explore things outside their comfort zone, and find new ways to communicate with others. If you've struggled with possessing talents, skills, and abilities that are unique or unusual, I invite you to find the encouragement you need as you follow Skye's journey from *believing* to *believing in*."

~Shell Vera

Author of *When I Stopped Remembering Tomorrow: Poetry & Reflections About Being Present*; Voice Discovery Coach

"My friend Donn King proves once again why he is one of my favorite storytellers. In his latest book, *Medium Well: The Journey*

From Believing - to Believing In, he weaves a fascinating tale of connecting with others in a most unconventional way. The characters are lovable, the narrative compelling, and I found myself wonderfully immersed in the theater of my mind. Oh, and I happened to learn some great life lessons too! Bravo, Donn King! Bravo!"

~ Jeff C. West
Award-winning coauthor of *Streetwise to Saleswise: Become ObjectionProof™ and Beat the Sales Blues*
and *Said the Lady with the Blue Hair: 7 Rules for Success Wrapped in a Wonderful Lesson for Life.*

♦♦♦

"A real page turner. You never know what the next page will bring? What? Who? When? Where? Super fun and exciting. One thing is for sure, though, the life and business lessons are profound."

~Yermi Kurkus
Author of *For The Love of Success* and co-founder of YKC Group

"People say that what we're all seeking is a meaning for life. I don't think that's what we're really seeking. I think that what we're seeking is an experience of being alive, so that our life experiences on the purely physical plane will have resonances with our own innermost being and reality, so that we actually feel the rapture of being alive." — Joseph Campbell in *The Power of Myth*

Chapter One

New Experiences

The little girl sat cross-legged in the hospital bed as Skye entered the Intensive Care Unit room, gazing at the purple stuffed dragon in front of her. She looked up, turning her solemn gaze to Skye. Skye smiled and waved, pushing her cart in front of her, but the girl showed no reaction.

"Sorry to intrude!" she said. "I'm just here to collect the trash and clean up a bit. Is that OK?"

The girl said nothing, continuing to watch Skye with vague interest. Skye shrugged. She went about her business, but kept talking since it helped diminish her own anxiety. Still new to the job, less than a week as an Environmental Services Technician ("Fancy word for 'housecleaning staff,'" she told her mother), she wanted to make a good impression. But she remembered similar friendly folks who made her feel better she was a patient here.

"Room hasn't changed much," she said. "The equipment is newer, of course, but I still remember that little alcove. I used to pretend it was an airlock, and I was on a spaceship. And that TV on the wall is *much* better than the one I had."

As she worked, Skye looked around the room, noting things that had not changed as well as new items.

The freestanding closet remained, with the same missing patch of laminate on the edge of one door. The blinds covering the fifth-floor window looked the same, though a new medical tower now blocked the view across the valley.

The pulse oximeter sounded the same *beep, beep, beep* she remembered, though touch-screen controls had replaced the knobs, and a shiny new monitor beside it tracked respiration, blood pressure, and several other lines and curves Skye didn't recognize.

The ventilator looked familiar, but the humidification chamber measured only one-quarter the size of the ones she had seen during her stay, fed by a continuous line from a bag of distilled water. By the door stood a laptop computer on a portable stand in front of a medication cabinet with dozens of drawers, protected by a keypad to track usage.

She moved the mop from her cleaning cart and began to set up for her routine.

"Have the volunteers brought you any DVDs to watch?" she asked. "Do they still even have those, or is everything streamed?"

She looked over her shoulder as she pulled the full trash bag filled with diapers and empty nutrition bottles. *Complete Pediatric*, she thought. She noticed the feeding tube running to what she knew was a G-tube or a GJ-tube and reminded herself not to talk about the food in the cafeteria.

The girl still silently gazed at her, a little quizzically. Skye turned toward her, since it felt rude to talk with her back turned.

"Frozen had just come out, if I recall, and I watched it so many times, my dad would shout at it, 'No! I don't want to build a snowman!' He really made me laugh with that."

"I saw that one for the first time here in the hospital," said the girl. "But only in pieces, since I had to watch it in between treatments."

"Me too! Frustrating, isn't it? You never get to watch a whole movie when you're in the hospital."

The girl stared open-mouthed at Skye for a moment, then said, "Can…. Can you hear me?"

Skye looked left to right, held her hands palm up, and shrugged. "Hello! Of course I can. I'm not deaf, you know. I thought you didn't talk, though."

The girl began speaking so rapidly that Skye couldn't follow the words. The girl appeared to be about 10 years old, but her speech sounded somehow more childlike and more mature, like that of someone Skye's own age. The girl got excited, waving her hands around so that Skye feared she would dislodge the IV in her wrist.

"Whoa, slow down!" she said, holding her hands up to signal a stop. "I can't keep up with that. Is there something I can get for you?"

"My name is Hope," she said. "What's yours?"

"Hi, Hope, but I have the advantage. I saw your name on the strip outside your door. So I'll come over so you can see my name badge, and we'll be even, OK?"

Skye stepped to the edge of the bed, and Hope squinted at the badge.

"I can't see all that well," she said. "They had to sew part of my eyelids shut to keep my eyes from drying out since I don't blink enough, and I sleep with my eyes open. What's it say?"

"It says, 'Skye Jackson.' My parents meant it to be an uplifting name, but I hated it in high school. All the boys thought it was funny to say 'Reach for the Skye' and try to hug me, but I didn't think it was funny."

Hope laughed. "It's not funny, but it's funny that they *thought* it was funny. Silly boys." The two laughed together.

"I didn't mean to gush all over you," Hope said, "but most people can't understand what I'm saying at all. In fact, you're the first person who has ever talked *with* me instead of *at* me."

"That's not very nice! I'm happy to talk with you. I'm just here to clean up a bit, but if there's something I can get for you, I'd be happy to."

"If you would, please, just pass on a message to Erica. She's my nurse today, she's great, taking good care of me, they all are, but she doesn't know that I'm hurting down here." Hope pointed to her lower right abdomen underneath the billowing hospital gown. "Can you tell her that there's something going on there? I think they may need to do an ultrasound, that's what they had to do before. I thought the pain would wipe me out last time before they figured out the problem."

"Sure! I'll be glad to pass that on, but you could have just pushed that button on your bed rail to tell her. I'm sure she would want to know."

Hope looked at the control array, almost longingly, but she didn't reach for it. "I can't push that," she said. "My dad usually does it if he notices something out of the ordinary, but he and Mom went down to the cafeteria a little while ago. I'd appreciate it if you would just find Erica."

"OK." Skye thought, *That button's in easy reach. But she hasn't reached for that stuffed dragon, either. Maybe she can't use her arms.* Skye finished gathering the bags she had pulled while they talked and put them in her cart. "I'll pass the message right along. See you later!"

"I hope so! Hope. See what I did there?"

"Good one! One thing's for sure, with you around, we always have Hope."

Hope rolled her eyes, and Skye could see the eyelids partially sewed together. "Where have I heard that one before?" They both laughed, and Skye left the room and crossed to the nurses' station that occupied the entire southwest corner of the unit so that each room faced it. She spotted Erica and waved at her.

"Hey, I hope I'm not getting out of my lane, but this patient just asked me to pass on a message to you. She said she had something going on in her lower right abdomen, and she thought she might need an ultrasound. Does that make sense to you?"

Erica stared at Skye for a moment, then looked over her shoulder and back at Skye.

"That patient? Room 509?"

"Yeah, I just came out of there. She asked me to pass it along, said she couldn't push the button. Hope."

Erica slowly shook her head. "Hope is a frequent flyer here. She has never spoken a word in her 20 years. She can't push a button because she doesn't move. You cannot possibly have had a conversation with her."

"I just did! Look, come in, let's make sure we're talking about the same patient."

The two of them went back into 509, Skye leading the way. The same girl lay on the bed—not sitting up, but prone, her legs slightly pulled up, her arms bent with each clutching a stuffed animal. At her feet lay the purple dragon.

"Hope? Are you awake?"

Hope had no response, though her eyes were open as much as her eyelids would allow, looking without focus at the ceiling. A small rivulet of drool drizzled from her mouth. Erica picked up the Yankauer suction tip and used it like a hummingbird sipping nectar. Hope never moved.

"There now, sweetie, that probably feels better," Erica said. She leaned in. "Have you been talking to Skye, and you didn't tell me first? Hmmm? You're going to make me jealous!"

Skye noticed Hope's heart rate jump about 10 points, but only for a few seconds before it settled back to its steady 72 beats per minute. Hope slowly closed her eyes.

"I'll check on you again in a few minutes, honey. You just rest."

Erica motioned toward the door, and Skye looked over her shoulder one more time, but Hope lay still, only the rise and fall of her chest giving any indication of movement.

Erica closed the door behind her and looked at Skye with some sympathy.

"Somebody told me you spent a couple of months here a few years ago."

"Yeah, that's right. Ten years ago or so, I guess."

"If you don't mind me asking, what brought you here?"

"I don't mind. I got struck by lightning. Singed my hair, blew off a couple of toenails. I don't need tattoos. I have some interesting lightning embroidery instead. They're called Lichtenberg figures."

Skye pulled up one leg of her scrubs to reveal a network of fine scars in an intricate, branching pattern ironically resembling lightning bolts, a lighter brown tone against her dark skin.

"I'm reminded every time I change socks. I spent two months here, mostly in that very room, 509. I've never forgotten the people who not only kept me alive but helped me to get back to normal."

"Wow. That's quite an experience! I'll bet it changed the way you look at things. Did it, um, well, did it have any, you know, mental health impact? If I'm not prying too much."

Skye hesitated. After all, she had only met Erica that morning. *Can I trust her? I don't know. But I need a friend here....*

"Well, it was a little traumatic. For a long time, I was scared to go outside. My parents homeschooled me after I got out of the hospital, and I had to talk to a counselor to deal with the anxiety. Um, why do you ask?"

"I don't mean to imply anything bad! But I had a friend once who had been struck by lightning, and he wound up having to get psychological counseling because he kept hearing voices from people who weren't there. Does that sound familiar?"

Skye pursed her lips, shook her head. "No, not really. Not at all. I have enough issues being afraid of things that are actually there—I don't think I could handle it if I heard things that weren't."

Now Erica hesitated, but after a moment she plowed ahead. "I'm not sure what to say here, but I have to tell you that there is no way you could have had a conversation with Hope. I mean, she didn't say anything to you just now, did she?"

"Of course not! She just lay there, staring at the ceiling. If she had said something, you would have heard it."

"I'm telling you, she's never said *anything* to *anybody*. Her dad told me that when she was a baby, she made the usual grunting sounds, a little babbling, but that dried up. She has a severe neurological challenge."

Erica crossed her arms, looked at the closed door of 509 again, then back directly at Skye. "He's a speaker, you know, or he used to be. He said his biggest unrealized dream was to hear his daughter's voice. So, I don't know who you were talking to, maybe you heard something on her TV, but it couldn't have been Hope."

***

Skye looked at her cell phone, but she didn't really see it. She scrolled aimlessly, as her thoughts ran around like startled butterflies. A casual observer would have thought she checked her social media like 90 percent of the other café patrons sitting alone or in pairs at the little tables, half of them in scrubs, taking their brief breaks in long hospital days.

What just happened? I talked to that child as clearly as I talked to Erica, but Erica tells me I couldn't possibly have had that conversation. Am I crazy?

She remembered when she had occupied a similar bed in that very room, though her memories came in flashes, with sizable gaps. She took her parents' word that she had spent two weeks in the ICU before regaining consciousness. To Skye, that time simply didn't exist, like the experience of going under anesthesia, counting down from 100, reaching 97, then suddenly waking up with the procedure completed and a complete absence of any sense of a time gap.

After the first two weeks, though, she drifted in and out of consciousness, and she remembered times when she must have been dreaming or hallucinating, with random children wandering into her room or sometimes floating in through the ceiling or coming up from the floor.

A young woman in a food service uniform suddenly sat in the chair across from Skye. "I hope I'm not intruding," she said. "I just have a few minutes, and all the other tables are full."

Skye looked around and saw that all the chairs were occupied, with a half dozen more people lined up at the single cash register. She smiled at the newcomer and said, "No problem! I won't be here long, anyway. Just waiting for a coffee."

"I know. I actually work behind the counter. It was time for my break, so I thought I would just bring yours over rather than ask you to wade through the crowd over there."

"Oh, thanks! That's very thoughtful."

Skye gratefully accepted the steaming paper cup enwrapped in its cardboard sleeve. "I just need to go add some sugar and cream. Gotta smooth it out a little!" She started to stand, but the young woman said, "I added sugar and cream already. I hope I did it right. Two sugar packets and two creams, French vanilla. Right?"

"Yeah, how did you know?" Skye sat down again, tentatively took a sip of just-right coffee, and tipped her head to the side as a smile built. "That's perfect!"

"I just started here last week. I know it's important to learn the regulars, and so I'm paying attention. I remembered that's what you got yesterday."

"Impressive. I've been working here a couple of weeks myself, but I still can't quite remember where the bathrooms are."

"There's one right around that corner." She pointed and smiled impishly. They both laughed. The newcomer stuck out her hand and said, "I'm Callie, by the way."

Skye took the proffered hand, gave it a single shake with a smile of her own, and said. "Skye."

"Pretty! I like that name. So, what do you do here, Skye?"

Skye pointed to her shoulder patch. "I'm an Environmental Technician. That means I clean stuff."

"Excellent! You and I may have the most important jobs in the hospital. You keep the place clean and safe. And I deal caffeine to keep people sharp and alert. What would they do without either of us?"

Skye raised her eyebrows and nodded. "I hadn't thought of it that way before, but you're right! They should be glad we're here!"

"Exactly. And I'll bet a lot of folks around you really appreciate you, especially when there's been an 'incident' in a room."

Skye leaned in. "Mostly, they don't even know I'm there."

Callie whispered, "I know what you mean. In fact, a lot of people forget I was ever even around."

"I can't believe that! You seem to have a way of instantly connecting with someone."

"True enough. Honestly, though, I don't care if people remember me. I just enjoy helping them to focus, give a listening ear, ask questions."

"Well, you have certainly helped me. In fact, I'm just realizing how much clearer I'm thinking now. I was really confused when I came in here, trying to fit my head around something that happened upstairs, my thoughts jumping all over the place! I still don't know what happened, but I don't feel my stomach churning any more."

"Good! I still have a few minutes—if you just want a listening ear to help you sort things out, I'm happy to do that. Only if you want to, of course."

Skye considered. She had opened up to Erica, needing to make connections in "the new job," and she wasn't sure whether it had been a good idea. She feared Erica might report her or something.

On the other hand, Callie had no influence over her job. *This could be a genuine help with no risk*, she thought. *What the heck.*

Skye told Callie all about her "conversation" with the girl who couldn't talk. When she got to the part where Erica dropped her bomb, she thought Callie might turn skeptic, but she just kept listening intently, nodding in all the right places, not interrupting, encouraging her to keep talking.

"So, what do you think happened there?" Callie asked.

"I have absolutely no idea. I have to admit, it makes me wonder if I imagined the whole thing."

"Imagination is certainly a powerful thing! Also, quite valuable!"

Skye sighed. "Mine gets me in trouble a lot. But it is what it is. Anyway, it is very nice to meet you! I'm afraid I let it get in the way of work, though. I was only supposed to be on a 30-minute break, and we have to have been here for at least an hour." She checked her watch, then raised her eyebrows. She tapped the watch twice. "Yep, the second hand is moving, but this can't be right. According to this, it's only been five minutes since I sat down here."

"Check the clock on the wall behind you."

"Wow! I guess sometimes time crawls when you're having fun."

"I had fun too! And I'm glad the coffee helped your focus. Enjoy the rest of your break, and I hope you can process whatever you're trying to figure out. See you tomorrow?"

"You bet!"

"One last thing." Callie reached into her pocket and pulled out a spiral notebook. Skye briefly wondered how it had fit, too big for the pocket. It had not stood out in its bulk before. But she quickly forgot about that as Callie held it out to her. The cover seemed to have depth to it as colors slowly swirled in the institutional lighting. "I thought you might like this," Callie said. "I have extras, and don't need this one. I sometimes find that writing thoughts down helps you to get a handle on them. Writing is a great thinking tool, in fact. So maybe this will help you with your cogitating."

Skye ran her hand across the smooth surface, opened the notebook to find a plain black pen tucked into a receptacle in the cover. Another optical illusion, since the pen had to be wider than the cover's thickness. *How cool!* she thought, then she beamed at Callie. "Thank you very much! I don't think I've ever had a nicer notebook and pen! I will certainly get good use out of these."

"You're welcome. Happy writing!"

Skye turned to the notebook as Callie slipped away. She opened to the first page and wrote at the top, "What the heck happened with that girl?" She chewed the end of the pen for a few seconds, and then started writing what had happened, her confusion around it, and her concerns. Time stood still. When the alarm on her phone went off, she had written three pages that had spilled out as smoothly as water from a faucet.

She sat back and skimmed over the three pages, looking for any patterns. When she reached the end of what she had written, she turned one more page and found a purple sticky note. She looked more closely at the elegant handwriting in ink that seemed to float off the page.

Writing is a great thinking tool. Ironically, it helps you master detail *and* see the big picture.

I wonder who wrote that? Skye thought. *Maybe Callie left me a note. I'll have to ask.* She frowned. *But how did she know how many pages I would write?* She shrugged to herself. *It's a good thought, anyway.* She turned the note over to see another line.

Don't just read the other side. Write it down yourself. That will make it your own.

Smiling to herself, she wrote it on the page where she found the sticky, closed the notebook and tucked it into her backpack, carefully setting it in one of the interior pockets to protect it, then ran for the elevator. Almost certainly somebody needed her in the ICU, and she determined to not let the day's "incident" distract her from her duties.

***

"Had any more conversations with patients?" Erica asked.

Skye had not heard her approach, so she jumped a little. She looked warily at Erica, but Erica's smile seemed friendly enough, so she smiled back.

"Not this morning," she said. "They've all been asleep except for the kid with the burns, and he seemed drawn into a Disney cartoon. Why?"

"Just wondered. I think it's cool that you talk with the kids is all. A lot of housekeeping folks just come in, pull the trash, mop the floor, and leave. These kids can feel a little isolated, seeing no one but Mom and Dad and medical types who want to poke and prod. I think it's good for them to have the human contact."

Erica hesitated, then asked, "Have you cleaned 509 yet?"

"No, just haven't gotten around to it yet."

"Can I be honest with you?"

Skye dropped back into wariness again. "Sure, I guess. But I'm nervous now."

"Don't be nervous! It's probably none of my business, but, well, I kind of knew you hadn't been in 509 yet. I thought I saw you sort of skip it, in fact. And I was a little afraid that thing yesterday has spooked you. Are you OK?"

They both looked at the closed door of 509. "Yeah, I'm OK, I guess, and I have to go in there at some point. I know y'all go through a lot of sheets and such for her. I just.... I don't know, I'm still sorting it out. You haven't told anyone, have you?"

"Not at all! Frankly, I don't want to lose you. People sometimes find cleaning the ICU extra challenging, but in the two weeks you've been here I can tell that you don't let the gross stuff get to you, and you work hard. Maybe you've been working too hard? Anyway, why would I tell anyone? This place is a gossip hotbed, but we're mostly talking about the other nurses and the doctors."

"Thanks. I just don't want to screw this up. I really need this job."

"Would you like for me to go in there with you?"

"No, no, I'm fine. I'll do that room next."

Erica smiled encouragingly. A call light went off over 514. "That's one of mine. See you later!"

Skye contemplated 509 again. With determination, she rolled her cart to just outside the door, stood there for a second, then knocked quietly, then louder, then she opened the door a crack.

"Housekeeping!"

No answer.

She slipped into the darkened room. Hope appeared to be sleeping, her pulse on the monitor in the high 50s. "I just need to pull the trash. Is this an OK time?"

No movement, no answer, no change in pulse. Skye pulled the blue trash first, checked the red, then pulled a flat mop from her cart and put a fresh microfiber on it. Hope's parents had not yet arrived, so this was a perfect time for tending to the floor.

When she finished with the floor, she propped the mop up against the large trash receptacle that formed the center of her cart, took a new package of paper towels from the end bin, and opened the nearly empty dispenser over the sink. As she tucked the new stack in, the handle of the mop slipped off the edge of the trash bin and hit the floor with a loud crack.

Instantly the dispenser, sink, cabinets, and wall disappeared, and Skye found herself holding the stack of paper towels out into empty air. Her eyes widened, and she looked side to side, frozen in place. Trees. Trees surrounded her, swaying in a light breeze, their leaves rustling as if whispering to each other. The paper towels slipped from her still raised hand and fluttered in the wind like so many butterflies.

"Are you actually here, or are you just part of my dream?" said a voice behind her.

Skye jumped forward as if struck by lightning again, turning in mid-air to face the voice, winding up about a foot off the ground. Hope stood there in her hospital gown, no sign of bed or wall behind her. Skye whipped her head to look left, right, down, her eyes wide.

"Wha... how.... What is happening?!?"

Hope walked to her, put out a hand devoid of an IV, and gently pushed Skye, who drifted back like a balloon on a string before returning to where she had hovered after jumping.

"You feel real. Sometimes, when I'm dreaming, Daddy comes to see me, and we talk, but he never remembers it when he wakes up. Or if he does, he never says anything about it. And sometimes I see him, but it's not really him, it's just me dreaming about him. I can tell, because when I try to touch him, my hand just goes through like I'm pushing through fog, and he doesn't talk to me. So, you feel real, but you're not talking to me."

Hope looked up at her and waited.

"I... I don't think you're dreaming me. But I don't know what's happening. Is this your dream? Why am I floating in the air?"

"Daddy flies around all the time. I think maybe most people fly around in their dreams. Are you asleep?"

"Not that I know of. I was cleaning your room, so unless I fell asleep standing up, no."

"I've never talked with someone who wasn't asleep, except for yesterday when you talked to me in my bed. But you weren't sleeping then either." Hope put her arms out as if spanning a doorway, then walked around in a circle, wagging her head from side to side. When she had come full circle, she looked up again at Skye and said, "Of course, I wasn't asleep then either. They came in to take more blood a few minutes ago, and I didn't like what they were doing, so I went to sleep. Daddy says when the going gets tough, the tough go to sleep. That's what I do."

The wind continued to blow through the surrounding leaves, and Skye drifted with the breeze. Tentatively, she put her arms out, moved as if she were swimming, and began to slowly move up into the sky. She realized she had come even with the treetops and looked down to see Hope smiling up at her. Hope waved, and when Skye waved back, she turned herself over like an aerialist somersaulting between trapezes.

"Whoa!" she exclaimed, "I didn't mean to do that!" She tucked her arms to the side, then swooped down before extending her feet like a duck landing right in front of Hope.

"I still don't know what's happening, but I have to admit that was fun. Why aren't you flying around?"

"I can if I want to. But while I'm asleep, I just want to walk and run. I don't get to feel the grass when I'm awake. This is my chance to feel what weight means. I hear my nurses say I weigh about 80 pounds. I don't really know what walking feels like—but I'll bet you don't really know what flying really feels like, do you? How could you, since you don't fly when you're awake?"

"I hadn't thought of that before. I do dream I'm flying sometimes, and when I wake up, I can remember that feeling. This feels that way. But about all I can remember is the feeling. I never remember much of what happens in my dreams, just that I dreamed."

"Maybe that's why Daddy doesn't remember when he wakes up. I remember things, but I never hear anybody else talk about their dreams, so maybe they just don't remember them."

Hope skipped in a circle around Skye and said, "I see people do that on TV sometimes. It looks fun, and here it feels fun."

"Do other people come here with you sometimes?"

"Sure! Sometimes they see me and sometimes they don't, but I can tell when they're dreaming or when I'm just dreaming *about* them."

Skye laughed. "Sometimes Mama comes to see me. We have big, long talks, but she never remembers them, I think. When I'm awake and we go to the doctor, I see Mama in a wheelchair like mine, only hers has a little motor so she can move herself. Somebody has to push mine. But when we're here, Mama and I walk and hold hands. She doesn't fly much when she's here. She just holds my hand. Or if Daddy is here too, then Mama and Daddy dance. But Daddy usually wakes up first, and then Mama dances by herself, and dances with me."

From the sky, a voice said, "I tried three times to get a good vein, but I just couldn't find one. She has so much scar tissue. I'm hoping you can manage it—we really need to check her blood gases, but her last IV blew out."

Hope looked up. "They're going to try again. That will probably wake me up. Come see me again, Skye? I like talking with you, and maybe you'll remember this after we wake up. Will you come again?"

Trees and grass and sky vanished. Skye stood in front of the sink, looking into the empty paper towel dispenser, the newly opened stack scattered on the counter and onto the floor.

"Oh, sorry, didn't see you standing there!" Skye recognized a phlebotomist from the ER across the bed, holding a butterfly needle in one gloved hand and Hope's wrist in the other. Nearer to her, a more familiar ICU phlebotomist turned and looked surprised. "Hi, Skye! You must have been standing there when I came in. You're so quiet!"

A glance at the monitor showed Hope's pulse running at 112, definitely awake. Skye surveyed the scattered paper towels, began picking them up. "Yeah, quiet, that's me! I should have said something. Let me get out of y'all's way."

Skye threw the paper towels in the big trash can and exited the room as fast as she could. She practically ran from the ICU and took the elevator straight to the ground floor under the main hospital. New job or not, she told her supervisor she had suddenly become sick and needed to go home. With her parents away on a vacation, she could have their house all to herself with all the comforts of a familiar place away from the dreariness of her little one-room apartment. She went straight to the bedroom they still maintained for her, buried herself in the sheets and comforter, and hoped if she dreamed, she would not remember.

***

Skye stayed in bed the whole day Thursday, only getting up long enough to go to the bathroom or heat a can of soup or leftover pizza. She spent a couple of hours writing in the notebook Callie had given her, trying to make sense of it all. She considered calling in sick Friday also, but her sense of responsibility and desire to make a good impression at the new job finally overrode her reluctance to go back into the unit.

Her phone chimed, and she saw in her texts it was her mom. "How's the new job going?"

Great, Mom, I may be losing my mind. I'm hearing from people who can't talk. Instead, she typed, "Great! Getting comfortable with the new routine."

Maybe they will have moved Hope down to the regular floor by now, she thought, although she knew the floors had few beds open and Hope's pneumonia persisted. *Maybe I can swap with someone, clean a different floor.*

But all the assignments had been made when she got to work around 7 AM. Bracing herself, she took her cart up the staff elevator and immediately set to work, first cleaning the recently vacated rooms, moving next to the staff-only area behind the nurse's station. With no parents around that early in the morning, the nurses chatted quietly but freely as Skye collected the trash cans and mopped the floor.

"It's one of the things I appreciate about Dr. Powell," said an older nurse Skye didn't recognize. "When I started nursing, it wasn't unusual for a doctor to effectively tell a nurse to shut up. If I offered any observation about what might be going on with a patient, he—and it was always a he—might ask when I got my medical license. But Dr. Powell listens if I see something I think he might not have picked up on. I know I'm not a doctor, and I'm never going to tell a parent what I think is happening with their child. But it's nice when the doctors recognize nurses have the best chance to spot those little details that could make all the difference."

"Absolutely," said another, sipping her coffee at a corner desk. "I mean, take yesterday. Erica told me she shared an observation about 509 that Dr. Powell took seriously. Although he saw nothing alarming, as a precaution he ordered an ultrasound, and that's when they found the blockage. If it hadn't been for Erica's confidence, that little girl could have had a rupture and a serious complication, especially since she can't tell us when she hurts."

Skye kept mopping, saying nothing, but her heart rate climbed. She longed to ask what happened, but she knew she had no legitimate interest, and she didn't want to let on that she had even heard. *Please let them keep talking,* she thought. She took a bottle of disinfectant spray from her cart and cleaned the counter just inside the little coffee alcove, well within earshot.

"She's your patient today, isn't she? 509? How did that turn out?"

"Night shift said she rested comfortably all night, and she certainly seems better today, though that right lung still has a shadow on the X-ray. Mom and Dad just went in there, and I know they're relieved. Nobody suspected the intestinal issue until Erica brought it up. I don't know how Erica noticed it, but I'm glad she did."

Skye finished behind the desk and took her cart out onto the floor. Part of her wanted to avoid 509 at all costs. Another part wanted to go right in.

She took a deep breath, let it out, and turned her cart toward the open door of 509.

Chapter Two

Exploring

Skye could see right into 509 as she approached. One of three rooms set up to allow isolation when needed, it had an outer entrance with its sink, cabinets filled with boxes of gloves and other equipment. Yellow isolation gowns hung on hooks, ready for donning, with an inner door leading to the actual hospital room.

Sliding glass doors fronted most of the rooms in the unit for maximum visibility from the nurses' desk, with thick curtains to pull when privacy was needed. The nature of the construction of the isolation rooms meant less external visibility. Even when both doors stood open, as they did now, you could not see the patient from the floor without entering at least the first door.

But walking straight in, Skye could clearly see Grace Roberts, Hope's mother, in her wheelchair sitting beside Hope's bed, holding her daughter's hand. Skye knocked on the door frame and said, "Housekeeping. Is this a good time to pick up your trash?"

Grace turned to Skye, smiled, and said, "Please! Come on in." As Skye moved into the room, she saw Dan Roberts, Hope's father, with his back turned as he hunted for something in the storage cabinet. He also turned and smiled.

"Let me get out of the way," he said. "I don't want to hamper your work."

"It's no problem! These rooms are all full of equipment, and we're used to working around in small spaces." She looked sideways at Hope, who lay still in the bed. "How's she doing today?"

"It's always hard to tell," said Dan. "Really, all we can do is check her stats and watch her facial expressions. Her face doesn't change much, but if something's bothering her, she can certainly grimace."

"I'm feeling *much* better since they worked on my tummy," said Hope.

Skye quickly looked from Dan to Grace. Neither of them registered having heard Hope. Grace had turned back to crocheting and Dan had continued talking, though his words sailed by Skye.

"...and so it's really fortunate they figured out about the intestinal thing. But thank you for asking! We appreciate all that you and your colleagues do to keep things clean and tidy. I know how hard it is to keep things clean in her room at home, and it must be that much harder in an environment like an ICU."

Skye didn't reply immediately. She was watching Hope sit up out of her body. Dan followed Skye's gaze, looked at Hope, back at Skye, and smiled uncertainly.

Skye could see Hope sitting up in bed, looking back at her, but a translucent version. Like looking through heavy fog, she could see a physical Hope still lying in the bed, eyes half open and rolled back, with a slender, misty cord, like an umbilical cord, connecting the two. Misinterpreting her gaze, Dan said, "It's hard seeing kids like her, I guess. You never get used to it, do you?"

"Hmmm? Oh, I'm sorry, I didn't mean to stare. It's just.... I'm fairly new to the job, but I'm used to the ICU. I spent a couple of months here about ten years ago, and after I came out of my coma, I got to know some of the other kids. And then I volunteered here, bringing movies and toys around to the kids to help pass the time. But.... Well, I've never seen a child quite like Hope."

"I'm not a child anymore!" said Hope. "Daddy says I'm 20, and that means I'm not even a teenager anymore!"

"Hope is definitely special in a lot of ways," said Dan, "not least because her condition is so rare. In fact, according to the only medical journal article we could find about it, there were only 15 to 20 cases like hers known at the time of the article."

He walked to the bed and squeezed Hope's ankle under the sheets, smiling sadly. "She ought to be in college by now, but she never had the chance. On the other hand, in a lot of ways, she's just like the rest of our kids. She's 20 now, so she'll age out of coming to this hospital soon." He leaned toward Skye and lowered his voice. "She may not be a teenager anymore, but she's definitely a mean-ager."

"Hey! I heard that!" Translucent Hope looked indignant, and Skye couldn't help but laugh.

"Just ignore him," said Grace. "He wishes she could be as mean as her older brothers and sisters, that's all."

Dan looked down, his eyes slightly moist. "That's true. Some of the older kids were hellions, but I would give anything if Hope could cause us more trouble than having to come to the hospital so often."

"Be careful what you wish for," said Grace and Hope at the same time. Hope giggled and said, "Daddy says great minds think alike whenever he and Mama say the same thing at the same time. I guess so!"

"Is... is it OK if I go say hi to her?" Skye asked.

"I don't see why not. I think she enjoys people talking with her."

"Some people, yeah," said Hope. "I *don't* like people who talk baby talk at me."

Hope walked around on the side of the bed closest to Grace so no one but Hope could see her face, and smiled down at physical Hope. She winked with her left eye, the one hidden from view.

"Hello, Hope. My name is Skye. We met earlier this week, but I didn't get to come talk with you."

Translucent Hope rolled her eyes, but physical Hope never moved. Translucent Hope stood up on the bed, then floated toward the ceiling, tethered by the almost transparent cord.

Without taking her eyes off physical Hope, Skye said, "Have you ever been able to interact with her at all? Maybe one of those 'blink once for yes, twice for no' things?"

"Lord knows we've tried," said Dan. "In the early days we tried using a picture board, hoping she could point, or maybe look at blocks with pictures or words so we could get her message. Either she couldn't or wouldn't, and mostly I think it just was beyond her capabilities."

"I tried," said Hope. "I used to get my stupid body to at least twitch or something, but I could never get the hang of it, and the older I get, the less I can get it to do. Ask him if he found a way to get a 'yes' out of me."

"So, if yes or no wouldn't work, were you able to find a way to get at least a 'yes'?"

"Funny you should ask. We found that sometimes we could ask a question in yes or no form, and if her answer was 'yes,' she would give us a slow blink. She doesn't blink her eyes much at all, but when she does, it tends to be a quick blink. We think that when she slowly closes her eyes and opens them again, it's on purpose."

"It's a lot harder since they sewed my eyelids partly shut," said Hope.

"I'll bet it's harder with her eyelids like that. How did that happen?"

Grace put her crochet down in her lap. "She doesn't blink enough. Plus, she sleeps with her eyes open, and then she wouldn't blink at all. Her eyes got so dried out, her corneas were scarring."

"It itched really bad, too," said Hope.

"It must have been uncomfortable for her, too," said Grace. "We noticed her pulse staying up, and couldn't find any other reason for it. Her eye doctor recommended sewing about a third of each eyelid together so the tears could lubricate more completely. I always have trouble remembering what they call it, but I think it's called a tarrsophagy. Dan? Is that right?"

"Tarsorrhaphy," said Dan. "Pretty close. I think it may have saved her eyesight, but it was sure hard seeing that done to my little girl. I guess it's not the worst thing she's gone through, what with the feeding tube and the tracheotomy and the rods in her back for the scoliosis."

"It's not," said Hope, "but it's one of the more annoying."

Skye burst out with a short laugh, and Dan looked puzzled. "Sorry!" Skye said. "I was just imagining that she might think it was pretty annoying."

Dan smiled. "I'll bet it was."

Skye looked once again at physical Hope's eyes, and said, "Hope, I'm wondering something. Is there anything I could do for you? If so, please give me a slow blink."

Translucent Hope reached down with ethereal fingers to physical Hope's eyelids, each hand's index finger appearing to touch an eyelid. She pulled down as if working a puppet, causing each eyelid to slowly lower and then pull up slowly to raise it.

"Look at that!" Dan said. "Now we just have to guess what it might be she wants."

"I want to change the channel on that TV," Hope said. "I've seen that movie a half dozen times."

"Would you like the channel changed on the TV?" Hope used her fingers on her eyelids again for a slow blink.

"You hit the jackpot first try," Dan said. "It could be a slow process to figure out what she wants to watch."

"Let's try this. Hope, I'm going to cycle through the channels. When you see something you want, give me a slow blink."

"That may or may not work," Dan said. "See, since we could never establish a signal for 'no,' the closest we could come was if there was no response. That could mean 'no.' But it could also mean she had fallen asleep, or she was ignoring me like any teenager ignores her parents, or maybe that I was asking the wrong question. I learned that if I got no response, I should turn the question over so it *could* be a yes instead of a no to the previous question."

"I see. So, like, 'Would you like to change the channel?' No response. Then, 'Would you like to leave the channel right where it is?' Then a slow blink would be the same as, 'No, don't change the channel.'"

"Exactly. You might get all the way through the channel lineup and get no response to any of them, but that might mean she fell asleep."

"I will not fall asleep!" Hope said. "It would be so much easier if I could just tell them what I want!"

"I'm willing to try," Skye said. "Let's just see what happens."

She began clicking the remote, watching physical Hope's face, with translucent Hope holding her fingers on her eyelids at the ready. She clicked slowly while translucent Hope watched the screen. On the fifth click, a familiar Pixar film was just getting started, and Hope said, "That's it!" She moved her eyelids up and down, and Skye said, "That seems to be the one!"

"I've never seen this one all the way through!" Hope said. "This is great! Thanks, Skye!"

"Well, I have a half dozen more rooms to clean, so I'd better get to it." She turned to physical Hope, gently touched her hair, and said, "Thanks for letting me visit with you, Hope. I'll come back and see you again, if that's all right with you and your parents."

"Please!" Hope said. "It's so much fun to have someone who actually hears me! But try to come back when they're not here, so you can really talk with me."

"Please!" Grace said. "I don't know if you noticed, but while you were talking with her, her pulse rate came down. She's more relaxed than I've seen her all day. I think she likes you. What's your name? They write the names of the nurses, doctors, and respiratory therapists on that white board, but they really ought to write your name too."

"Skye. My name is Skye."

"Well, Skye, my name is Dan, and this is my wife, Grace. And if I may, I'd really like to shake your hand."

Skye shyly put her hand out, and Dan shook it. "Now I can truly say I reached for the Skye," he said.

Both Grace and translucent Hope rolled their eyes, and both said, "Ignore him."

Skye laughed out loud. "I've heard it before, but not so confidently delivered. I'm working again tomorrow. I'll come see Hope."

She picked up the blue bag of trash, but turned as she reached the door. "And remember," she said, "it is absolutely certain that no matter what, you can say with confidence that you have Hope. Wokka, wokka, wokka!"

Dan looked surprised, then smiled. "A fellow punner! Double points for you. See you tomorrow!"

As Skye left the room, she turned to see translucent Hope waving to her. She waved back and quickly left the room.

***

What the heck are you doing?

Am I talking to myself now, or is someone else talking to me?

Skye had never felt so confused. When she had been in the room with Hope and her parents, hearing a ghost girl that no one else could hear had seemed as natural as any conversation could. She almost felt like a co-conspirator, keeping the conversation with the girl just between the two of them. Now, thinking back on it, she realized just exactly how bizarre the situation was.

Seeing ghosts? Was it a ghost? After all, she isn't dead. Am I? Am I imagining it all? Am I imagining this?

Skye held out her left arm, looked at it for a moment, then pinched herself.

"Ouch!" Either she could imagine pain effectively, or she was fully awake.

Maybe I should talk to someone.

"You look like you could use some company," said a voice behind her. Skye turned to see Callie standing there, holding two steaming cups of coffee.

"Funny. I was just thinking maybe I needed to talk to someone, but it may need to be a psychiatrist."

"Well, baristas can serve that function, sort of like bartenders without the alcohol. But you know the hospital has people on staff to provide a listening ear when you need it. They usually work with doctors or nurses because of the stress of their jobs, but the service is open to all of us."

"I remember them saying something about that during orientation. I just never thought it would be me needing it."

Callie set a cup in front of Skye, then took a seat across from her. "I appreciate the support that mental health professionals give. I have several sisters who work in similar fields, and although I don't pretend to be a therapist, I have found that a combination of coffee and a listening ear can work wonders. I'm on a break just prior to the lunch rush, so if you trust me, I don't mind listening, if that would help."

Trust, thought Skye. *I'm not sure* who *to trust. Could be a mistake to trust anyone. They might lock me up.* But somehow, although she had only met Callie yesterday, Skye felt as if they had known each other for years.

"Promise you won't tell anyone?"

"Who would I tell? But I can guarantee I won't tell anyone without your permission. Like I said, baristas are like bartenders for sober people. We know how to keep secrets. And make those swirly designs, but that's another skill set."

She smiled, and all of Skye's hesitations evaporated. After all, she had already told Callie about the conversation with Hope on Tuesday, and she had neither run nor turned her in to supervisors.

"You helped me a lot the other day, and I've been journaling in the notebook you gave me. So, yeah, if you don't mind...."

"Happy to help. Spill it."

Skye told Callie all about the morning. The news about Erica passing on what turned out to be a real medical concern. Hearing Hope talk while her parents couldn't hear. Trying to not react to the things Hope said. Helping to make Hope's experience a little better by finding a TV channel for her. How natural it felt then, how crazy it felt now.

Callie listened intently, nodding, holding eye contact. Nothing seemed to surprise her. It was almost as if she already knew, but she also knew Skye needed to talk it out.

"So that's what's been going on. I have no idea what to do next. Do I keep visiting Hope, even though it's not my job? What happens when she goes home? Like, have I made things harder for her in the long run? Is this just me remembering what it was like to be in the ICU? Am I getting too close to these kids?"

"Kids? Have you had an experience like this with any other kid?"

"No. Oh, I talk to all of them. I not only remember being a patient here, I remember the joy of volunteering, bringing them games and even playing with some of them. But I'm *really talking* to them. When they talk back, other people in the room hear them."

Skye paused, then said, "Come to think of it, every kid in the unit is fully conscious, except for Hope. Maybe that's the difference."

"They all sleep sometime, don't they? Have you ever seen any of them in your dreams?"

"To tell you the truth, I can't remember. I rarely remember my dreams. Although there was this one thing that happened Wednesday...."

Her phone chimed. "Oh, great. It's my mom, wanting to know how things are going. I can't tell her what's happening! How could I even begin?"

"I'm sure your mom is just worried about you."

"Yeah, but it's kind of annoying. She's been really protective ever since the lightning thing. But it's *really* annoying with all that's been going on. I'll send her something later. Wait until you hear what happened next!"

Skye told Callie about the "waking dream" she had had in Hope's room, about Hope walking while Skye flew through the trees. Since she tended to not remember her dreams, she had written about it in the notebook Callie had given her as soon as she could. She pulled it out now to read about the experience.

"But I don't think I was really asleep," she concluded. "I think Hope was asleep, and maybe I got pulled into her dream. It sounds weird when I say it that way. I remember it as clearly as I'm talking with you right now, but usually I can only remember that I had a dream. If I've had any of the kids in my 'real dreams,' I don't remember it."

They sat together in silence for a bit, then Callie said, "You want to know what I think?"

"If you think I'm crazy, I'm not sure I want to know." Skye smiled, but she also looked concerned.

"I don't think you're crazy. I think you're sensitive. I think you have an ability that few people do. I have known some people like that who became writers or actors or counselors. I've known some who wrote songs, and others who tuned instruments. Some have become veterinarians. I think you have a way of *tuning in* that you're just now discovering.

"So I think you should let me introduce you to someone I know. She comes here for coffee a lot. She's one of those people we talked about earlier who help hospital folks deal with stress. Only, I don't think you're dealing with stress. And she's not a psychiatrist. She's a social worker."

"Oh, great. One of those people who would be a psychiatrist if they could afford to go to school for 15 years. Is she going to ask me how I feel about this?"

"You sound like you've had some history with folks like that."

Skye pulled out the spiral notebook, flipped through the pages where she had written her experiences of the week. *This is going to take more than a social worker.*

"After I got struck by lightning, they had me work with a social worker that my dad's insurance would pay for. They were afraid I would be traumatized. So, yeah, I got a little tired of her constantly asking, 'And how does that make you feel?' It was like a broken record. How did I feel? Like you never know what can happen to you, like you're minding your own business and suddenly something can just zap out of the sky and try to kill you, like just any second everything can change."

Skye realized she was obsessively clicking the pen and stopped herself. "I'm scared, Callie. I don't know what's happening to me. I don't know why I'm imagining things, or even *if* I'm imagining things. I'm scared of what imagining stuff like that could mean. If I'm not imagining it, if it's really happening, I'm even *more* scared. I'm scared nobody will believe me. If they don't, the *best* thing that is likely to happen is that I lose my job, and that could derail everything I'm trying to do. The *worst* thing would be for them to lock me up in a psych ward."

Callie reached out and laid a hand on Skye's arm. Instantly, Skye felt a wave of peace roll over her. She looked up into Callie's eyes, and it felt like a warm sea enveloping her.

"I believe you, Skye," she said. "I believe *in* you. But I'm fairly sure you don't believe in yourself. And that's why I want you to talk with Irene. Let me see your notebook for just a minute."

Skye passed the notebook with its shimmering color cover across the table. Callie took the pen from its receptacle in the cover and turned straight to the next blank page. She wrote briefly, then passed the notebook and pen back.

"There's her email address and phone number. Call her this afternoon. You're off tomorrow, right? Irene actually works this weekend, so you could visit with her tomorrow without having to worry about a work schedule, and I'll bet she will have time available."

Skye looked at what Callie had written—a name, email address, phone number, and a quick sentence that read, "Sometimes talking with someone else helps you hear yourself more clearly." The handwriting looked familiar, and Skye started to ask Callie if she had written her the note last Tuesday. But before she could, Callie again laid a hand on Skye's arm, and again she felt peace. "Do this, Skye. Do it for yourself. And, in a way, do it for me. OK?"

"OK."

As Callie pulled her hand away, Skye once again noticed the tattoo on her right wrist. She had seen it before, but had paid little attention. This time, it seemed almost to dance above Callie's skin, like the ink on the page of her notebook.

"I don't mean to pry, but can I look at your tattoo?"

Callie laid her hand down on the table, palm up, so Skye could get a good look. She scrutinized it. "It looks like Greek. What does it say?"

"You're right, it is Greek, a vernacular called *koine*. It says '*poiesis*.' It's the basis for the English word 'poetry.' It doesn't *mean* 'poetry,' though. It means 'creativity.' I like having it right there, because it reminds me of the thing that is most important to me, what I help people with."

"It's really cool! It's so crisp, so simple and yet so meaningful. I've always wanted to get a tattoo, but I've never been sure of what."

Skye only noticed the room had been completely quiet for a long time when the normal noise and chatter returned. She looked around and realized the lunch crowd was coming in.

"I have to get back to it," Callie said. "Don't forget. Call Irene this afternoon."

"I will! Really! And I have to get back to it as well. Those trash bins won't empty themselves!"

***

As she sat in her parents' kitchen, Skye started to dial Irene's number for the third time, then clicked the delete button to wipe it out before sending for the third time.

Can I really trust her? Sure, social workers know how to keep a confidence, but she works for the hospital. What if this goes in my HR record? But it sounds like she maybe could help.

Skye dithered another 10 minutes. She still had the house to herself, so she had slept in later than usual, and was now enjoying a bowl of oatmeal with ginger peach tea. While she sipped the tea, she pulled out her shimmery notebook and flipped through the most recent pages, looking for some direction. That's when she noticed at the bottom of the last page, after her last note, an entry in handwriting different from her own.

"What are you waiting for? Make the call!" Followed by three hearts and what looked like a Greek word, εἰρήνη.

Skye looked at that last word, tried to remember the Greek alphabet, then realized she had Google Translate on her phone. She held the phone up and focused on the word, and saw an English translation of "peace." But then the screen shifted, and the word changed to read "Irene."

Curious, Skye typed a query into a Google search that said, "What does the name 'Irene' mean?" The first hit said, "From

Greek Εἰρήνη (Eirene), derived from a word meaning 'peace'. This was the name of the Greek goddess who personified peace." *Greek goddess?* She flipped to Wikipedia and looked up, "Eirene (goddess)." The entry said, "She is usually said to be the daughter of Zeus and Themis."

I guess that's a good omen. But who left me that note? Skye shrugged. Maybe Callie had written it when Skye wasn't paying attention. The Greek thing was a little odd, but after all, Callie had that Greek tattoo.

She sighed, picked up the phone and dialed a fourth time.

"Hello, this is Irene Duguid."

"Hi, Irene, my name is Skye Jackson, and I'm a fairly new employee of the hospital, and I'm working in the ICU, and I'm afraid it's stressing me in unhealthy ways, or something like that, and I just need to talk to somebody, and Callie in the café said I should talk to you, that you would be good and understanding and you wouldn't tell anybody, and can I come talk to you? Soon?"

There was a pause after the torrent, and just as Skye thought they had lost the connection, Irene said, "Wow, that's a lot, and it *does* sound like we probably ought to talk. Are you at the hospital today?"

"No, I'm off today, but I could be there in half an hour."

"Don't rush. Why don't you come by right after lunchtime, say 1 PM. Will that work?"

"Easily. Thankyouthankyouthankyou!"

"It's fine, hon. Just breathe. We'll have a nice conversation and help you figure out what's going on."

Skye hung up, sat for a minute, checked her watch. *Plenty of time*, she thought. *I just hope Irene lives up to her name.*

***

Skye didn't know what she expected from a hospital social worker's office, but whatever it was, Irene's office was different.

The bright light from the window featured a sky blue wall unlike the drab institutional paint of most offices. A desk faced the window, butting up against the windowsill so the light flooded the desk and the rest of the room. A thick rug of Persian design adorned the center of the room, covering an elegant hardwood floor. A coloring book and pencils lay in the middle of the rug alongside a potted plant, but otherwise the area felt open and warm, inviting.

On the wall next to the desk, Skye could see photographs of children and a framed print that looked like the product of a huge Spirograph. A small shelf held knickknacks and mementos, with wooden drawers and filing cabinets complementing the shelves filled with neatly arranged binders.

On the far end of the spacious office, things stood in chaotic contrast to the area around the desk, with winter jackets draped over a chair like you would see in a doctor's waiting room, education certificates and diplomas haphazardly tacked to the wall, and shelves overflowing with papers.

Irene turned from the desk in her blue leather swivel chair, smiled, and motioned toward the couch. Of course, there would be a couch—but this one reminded Skye of the one in her parent's living room instead the stereotypical counselor's.

"Have a seat!" Irene said, her manner as open as her gesture.

Skye immediately liked her and felt relaxed. Long, greying hair falling gracefully around her shoulders framed Irene's face. Skye guessed she might be in her mid-40s. She wore an array of colorful necklaces that vibrantly blended with the intricate patterns and designs of a cozy sweater, hoop earrings, and an eclectic collection of rings on her fingers.

Skye sat down and felt even better, supported by the couch and comfortable enough to spend an afternoon. She reached into her backpack and took out the notebook Callie had given her.

"Is it OK if I take some notes while we talk? I've been learning that writing things down helps me to process them."

"Sure, no problem. Whatever helps you, helps you. So, tell me a bit about who Skye Jackson is. What brought you to work here at Foothills Children's Hospital?"

"You mean beyond needing a job somewhere, anywhere? I'm in my first year of college, going to the community college because the money goes further. My parents make too much money on paper for me to qualify for financial aid, and though I got a scholarship or two, it's not enough to cover everything."

"I'm sure that's true, but what I'm asking is why work in this particular place? I'm not sure it pays any more than the typical job a college student gets at a fast food place, and it seems to be a lot harder. Looks like it would be easier to schedule classes around a different job, for instance."

"To be honest, I've missed class a few times because of scheduling conflicts and sometimes from just being too tired to go to class. But while I need the job to pay for school and living expenses, I wanted something more than *just* a job. Foothills Children's saved my life in a very real way."

"This sounds interesting! Tell me more."

"About 10 years or so ago, I got struck by lightning while I played softball. It wasn't raining or anything, just a little cloudy. Nobody really expected any danger, otherwise they would have cleared the field. Anyway, I don't remember anything about it, but my parents say I was by myself in the outfield when they saw a bright flash and I fell down with smoke coming off me. I was in a coma for a couple of weeks and spent two months in the ICU. I'm lucky to be alive. It could have stopped my heart for good—that's what happens to a lot of people who get struck.

"The folks in the ICU made all the difference to me. I wouldn't be here without them. When I was 17, I volunteered here with Child Life for a couple of years. I remember how much they helped me pass the time and deal with the whole situation when I was a patient here. I'm thinking about becoming a nurse or a PA or something, and so I figured that a job that lets me see 'behind the scenes' will help me decide if I really want to do that."

"Interesting!" Irene said. "I can certainly tell this is more than just a job for you. You know it's unusual for our environmental folks to talk much with patients, right? Nothing prohibits it, but I think most workers want to get in quietly and unobtrusively, do their jobs, and get out."

"That actually makes a lot of sense, since most days I don't have time for conversation. The work load varies, but I can bet I'll have to deal with at least 15 or 20 big bags of regular trash and an equal number of biohazard bags, plus taking care of the floors, cleaning up after spills, that sort of thing. Fortunately, I don't have to run the ride-on scrubbers. They look fun, but I could just see myself taking out a wall with one of those, and they have a guy who spends the whole day doing that, anyway."

"Do your conversations put you behind? Could that get you in trouble?"

"It could get me in trouble if it happened, but it doesn't, not really. I've gotten good at carrying on a conversation while I keep working. Sometimes, it seems like I've spent a long time in a particular room, and then I'll check the clock and find that I've only spent ten minutes in there. In fact, that's happened several times in one particular room, and that's part of what brings me to you today."

Irene nodded and waited patiently for Skye to continue, unhurried, completely focused. Skye noticed she had no notebook or any other way of tracking the conversation, giving Skye her full attention. It felt like talking with her favorite aunt.

Skye recounted the story of her first day with Hope. When she reached the part where Erica said Hope had never spoken a word, Irene raised her eyebrows, but she said nothing and kept listening. Skye plowed ahead with the story of the "dream sequence," as she thought of it. She pulled the spiral notebook out of her backpack and read what she had written immediately afterward. When Irene still made no comment beyond, "And then what happened?" Skye recounted the conversation in which she could hear Hope, but no one else could, or so it seemed.

"I told Callie all about this, too, and thank God she didn't think I was crazy. At least, I don't think she did. Although she told me to come talk to you, so maybe she *does* think I'm crazy." She paused, then looked tentatively at Irene. "Am I?"

Irene smiled warmly and said, "I don't like to call anybody crazy. I prefer 'reality challenged.'" This time Irene paused, then her smile quivered before they both burst out laughing.

"'Reality challenged.' I like that! I have never been accused of being too tightly bound to reality."

"Me neither!" Irene said. "I think reality is overrated. I am a little concerned about *your* reality, though."

Skye suddenly turned serious.

"No, don't worry! I don't mean you didn't experience what you experienced. I've experienced things myself that are hard to explain, and I don't doubt you a bit. My concern is how you process it. Do you doubt yourself?"

"Sure! I wouldn't be here if I didn't."

"That makes sense. So, ultimately, what do you want to learn from this? What do you want to know?"

"I want to know if what I experienced is real."

"Not to be too esoteric or philosophical or anything, but what do you mean by real? Obviously, other people aren't experiencing the same thing you are in the same situation. What would make it real? How would you know?"

"Hmmm. That's a good question. Well, for one thing, Hope told me she had a specific pain in a specific place, and it turned out to be true. If I was imagining it all, the things she told me wouldn't be true, right?"

"That could indicate that you have an ability to sense things with patients, and it manifests to you as if in a vision or a conversation. If so, that's a genuine ability that could serve patients, but you might not be having an actual conversation. Our minds can do amazing things sometimes."

"So that wouldn't be exactly crazy—or 'reality challenged.' That would just be the way my mind presented to me something I sensed?"

"Maybe. Not saying it is or isn't, just a possibility. My actual concern is this: do you believe in yourself? That's not always a good indicator. Schizophrenic people who hear voices telling them to jump off a bridge, for instance, should pay attention to those voices but not act on them. But I sense nothing like that from you. So, rather than asking if I believe you, let's turn it around: do *you* believe you? Your belief in yourself is more important than whether someone else believes you."

"I'm going to have to think about that one for a bit!" She wrote in her notebook:

> Your belief in yourself is more important than whether someone else believes you.

Skye thought back over her experiences from the entire week. She pressed her lips together and said, "It's as real to me as any other conversation I've had this week, with Callie, with Erica, with you. If I can't believe the conversation I had with Hope, I can't believe *any*thing happening to me. If I imagined that, then maybe I'm making you up right now!"

Irene held up an arm and pinched herself. "Ouch! If you're making me up, you're doing a really good job!"

Skye laughed. "You know, you're not quite like any other counselor I've talked to—not that there have been a ton of them."

A soft smile flitted across Irene's face. "I guess you could say I'm not the most conventional. In any case, you're talking about the Matrix paradox. How do you know any of your experiences are real and not just the result of some incredibly intricate virtual or simulated reality? The Matrix movie franchise delved into that in interesting ways, but people have been questioning their experience of reality since at least the time of Plato."

Irene paused as Skye wrote more in her notebook, then continued.

"I've told you I've experienced things I couldn't explain, but I've taken comfort in something I heard from one of my teachers. Dr. Corky Harrison used to say, 'Reality behaves as if it is out there.'"

"So, what should I do?"

"Let's keep talking, you and me. And in the meantime, keep a guideline in mind: if you ever have a conversation with Hope or someone like Hope where they try to get you to do harm, back away from that. Anything else, listen. Listen to the conversation, but listen to your heart as well. See if something useful comes from it."

Irene took out a business card and wrote on the back. "Keep this with you. It's my cell phone number. I rarely give that out, but I have a feeling that it may help you to know you can text me or even call me anytime. I have a feeling...." She trailed off, then said, "Just keep that with you. And listen to yourself."

Skye wrote in her notebook,

Listen to yourself. Listen to your heart.

She turned to the bookshelf to her right and pulled a book from it. "If you're interested in simulation theory, you might get something practical from this book, *Reality+*, by David Chalmers. Why don't you dig through this a bit and bring it back next week? Maybe we could meet on Friday?"

Chapter Three

In the Deep End

Erica met Skye at the employee's entrance to the ICU just as she arrived at the unit.

"This may sound odd," she said, "but I wish you would start with 511 today. Their trash needs pulling, and that's the official reason I'm asking you to go in there, but just between us, I think he could use one of your 'special visits.'"

Skye crossed her arms and looked warily at Erica. "Are you sure? I don't have any training for this."

"I just know I've seen Hope do really well after you've visited her. This boy is the first unconscious trauma patient we've had since all this started. If you can really do what it seems you can do, you can help him. But I'm not going to tell you anything about him, or show you any of his records. In the first place, I'm not supposed to, HIPAA and all that. In the second place, if you can really do this, he can tell you what happened to him."

"I can't guarantee anything. But I'm willing to give it a shot. The trash needs tending to, anyway."

The name tag by the door said "Charlie" in decorative hand-written script. The boy sat up in the bed as Skye entered, despite the "unconscious" label. Skye realized that, like Hope, he appeared translucent, insubstantial, while a more solid version lay still on the bed.

"You must be Charlie."

"Why won't anybody talk to me? You're the first person who acts like they can even see me or hear me!"

"Well, Charlie, it may be hard to wrap your head around, but chances are nobody else *can* see you or hear you. Do you know where you are?"

"I don't remember how I got here, but it looks like a hospital, and there are all these people who look like doctors and nurses around. They listen to my chest and shine lights in my eyes, and they talk to each other like I'm not even here."

"Where are your parents?"

He looked down. "They're both dead," he said. "I live with my grandmother, and I don't know where she is."

Skye's expression softened, and she said, "I'm sorry, Charlie. I don't really know why you're here either, but I'll help you find out. What do you remember?"

Charlie thought for a few seconds and then told Skye about having spent an afternoon with friends riding ATVs in woods near his house. He remembered topping a hill to find himself flying suddenly into a roadbed, and then nothing until he woke up in the hospital.

"Here's the thing, Charlie," Skye said. "As nearly as I can tell, you sort of woke up, but you also sort of didn't. I want you to slowly turn around in the bed, look behind you, and tell me what you see."

Translucent Charlie turned, almost as if swiveling on a stool, and saw his body with eyes closed and a feeding tube going into his nose. The pulse on the monitor immediately spiked, and he shot toward the ceiling, then bounced back closer to his physical body as the cord connecting them pulled like a long rubber band.

"What's that? Is that a hose or something? Why is it floating like that? Why am *I* floating?"

"All I can tell you is that I've seen that before on somebody else. I think it has something to do with keeping you and your body together. Otherwise, well, I don't know, but maybe you might float away."

Translucent Charlie reached down and patted himself on the chest and stomach, then stared at his unconscious form. "I... That.... I don't understand. Am... am I dead?"

"Honestly, I don't understand either, but I know that part of you is awake and having this conversation with me, and part of you is unconscious. I know other people can't see or hear the part of you that's awake, and I don't know why I can, but I can. And I can tell you without any doubt that you are not dead."

"What happened to me?"

"I don't know that part. I'm not a nurse. I'm just an Environmental Technician."

Charlie turned back to gape at her. "Oh, great. The only person who can see me is the janitor."

Skye bristled. "More than a janitor, thank you. I'm responsible for keeping people like you safe. Do you have any idea how easily disease can spread in a hospital?"

"Can you do anything to actually make me better? Can you help me wake up? No? Then what good are you? Anybody can haul trash."

"Sure, anybody can haul trash. But not everybody can talk to people like you. How about if I get one of the nurses to come in and tell you what happened, and I can pass on questions you have? Do you think that might be worth something?"

Charlie looked contrite, and said, "I would like that."

"Hold on."

Skye went to the door and looked over at the nurse's station. Erica sat facing the room, working on paperwork but closely watching. She looked up at Skye, who gestured for Erica to join her.

"Charlie wants you to tell him what happened."

"Oh, that's a cheap way to find out. Is that a psychic trick?"

"He doesn't remember what happened after the ATV ran into the road. He wants to know what happened after that."

Erica looked stunned. "How did you know about the ATV thing?"

"He told me, silly. But he doesn't know what his injuries might be, or how he got here, or where his grandmother is. He knows his parents are dead, but he didn't tell me why. Did you know that?"

"I knew his grandmother is his only next of kin, so I assumed his parents were out of the picture."

"Well, what you do know is the medical stuff. So come on in and tell him what's going on, and I'll tell you about the questions he has. Deal?"

Erica came to the side of the bed beside the prone body. "Charlie, my name is Erica, and I'm your nurse today. It feels a little odd talking to you when it looks like to me you're completely out if it. I feel a little foolish. How do I know you're hearing me?"

"He says he's floating toward the ceiling, and he can hear you fine, and you need to assume he hears you. Maybe then you won't talk to the blood lady about your date last Saturday. Charlie says he's seen things like that on the Internet, but he didn't want to hear about it."

Erica blushed a deep crimson. "OK, I guess you can hear. Where do I look when I talk to you? I can't see you."

"He has settled onto the bed now, so you can just talk to what you see. You're not going to make eye contact no matter what, so just tell him as best you can."

She then explained the extent of his injuries, how the doctors were treating them, how long he had been there. Through Skye, he asked some questions about medical terms.

Then Skye looked at Erica, hesitated, and said, "Charlie wants to know if he's going to come out of this."

Erica and Skye looked at each other silently. Erica said, "I shouldn't be talking about this stuff in front of you. HIPAA and all that."

Skye laughed. "Charlie said he doesn't know what a hippo has to do with anything, but he wants to know."

"So, Charlie, I'm not a doctor, but under the circumstances, I don't think we should try to get a doctor in here to 'talk' with you. While I'm not qualified to give a prognosis...." Erica hesitated again, well outside her comfort zone. But she plowed ahead. "From everything I can see, I think it's just a matter of time before you recover. You're going to have some challenges ahead of you, probably need some serious physical therapy and such. But as long as we can keep you from developing pneumonia, you should be fine."

"Charlie says thank you. And he also said not to let that guy get under your skin. He's a douche." Skye raised her eyebrows, and said, "Girlfriend, you are going to have to tell me about that sometime."

"He's not worth talking about." She turned to Charlie, softened, and said, "Thank you, Charlie. I'm glad Skye could connect us. We'll take good care of you."

The pulse on the monitor slowed. Skye said, "He's asleep now. Let's get out of here. I'm not sure I want to risk falling into the dreams of a 13-year-old boy."

***

Skye felt both elation and exhaustion. Although she had always wanted to help children for a career, she had never expected to do so the way she now had. But she found it took a lot of energy. After leaving the ICU, she sought some quiet time, but as soon as she sat down with a cup of break room coffee (*nowhere near as good as what Callie brings me*), her phone buzzed with a message from her supervisor.

"Where have you been? We're getting complaints about trash piling up."

Uh, oh. I'd better get back up there. Not only had she fallen behind in her cleaning duties, but between her work and her exhaustion, she had missed several of her college classes. *I don't want to get fired, and I don't want to flunk out.* She had started the semester with such enthusiasm, but the events of the last week had overshadowed her academic work. She couldn't believe mid-term loomed. She briefly considered taking off for the afternoon to catch up on academic work, but decided she need to take care of her job first.

She quickly went down to the ground floor to retrieve her cart, then headed back to the ICU. She steeled herself against getting pulled in to either Hope's or Charlie's conversation, but they seemed asleep. *Maybe they're playing together in dreamworld,* she thought, and wondered how much Charlie would remember, briefly saddened at the thought that he would remember nothing and that she had no way to know what Hope might remember.

She had already cleaned rooms 501 and 502, and 503 sat empty and unused. 504, however, required a thorough cleaning from top to bottom, having recently discharged a patient with avian flu. Skye had to swab all surfaces with disinfectant, wipe down the mattress, mop the floor twice (once for standard cleaning, a second time with disinfectant), change out the linens, empty all three trash containers, disinfect the sink, and even thoroughly wipe down the TV and DVD player.

After two hours in that room, she planned to break for lunch. But her supervisor texted her once again. "Looks like the trash is piling up in two-thirds of the ICU. Do you need help?"

She quickly texted back, "No, I've got it. Thanks!" She would have welcomed the help, but she didn't want to look incompetent. Sky knew her performance was under scrutiny, and she wanted to pull it off by herself, even though it meant missing lunch. With a sigh, she rolled her cart to 505 and began quietly working her way around the multiple family members surrounding a screaming toddler to gather trash, mop as best she could, and resupply the paper towels.

After that, she fell into a routine for the rest of the floor. She finally finished 518, looked back down the row with a feeling of satisfaction, and prepared to take a late lunch as a reward. She glanced at her phone, saw that the hospital cafeteria would close in 10 minutes. She put her cart in the back area, planning to secure it later, hoping to have just enough time to make it before they closed the cafeteria doors.

Her phone buzzed with a text message.

She considered ignoring it, but her sense of responsibility got the better of her. She groaned. "ICU called. Parent spilled something in kitchen. Please respond to it ASAP. Mop & bucket job. May be sticky."

One thing after another. She snagged a small bucket from her cart and a mop along with a bottle of cleaner for good measure, and headed for the kitchen.

***

The vending machine seemed intent on frustrating Dan. It appeared to accept his check card, but refused to complete the transaction.

Dan tried a different card, but got the same result, icon spinning on the small screen as it tried to process the card, followed by a timeout message. He looked at the package of cheese crackers taunting him on the other side of the glass. He didn't trust putting actual coins in, since the machine had more than once taken his money without delivering a product, but he realized even if the card processor worked, nothing guaranteed it wouldn't charge the card and fail to deliver.

Worth a try, he thought, and fed a couple of dollar bills into the machine. It rewarded him with whirring and clicking, followed by dropping the product into the delivery chute.

"Yes!" he said out loud. "Score!"

Funny how the little things can become so big in the hospital.

He took his prized crackers, along with a diet soda and a chocolate bar, to one of the small tables in the little family kitchen. Over the years Hope and her family had frequented this hospital, Dan had gotten quite familiar with the support options. He had spent many nights sleeping fitfully on institutional chairs that pulled out like Lazy Boy chairs without the charm, finding ways to get food during the times the cafeteria closed, doing a few loads of laundry, squeezing in shower time, packaging food in the shared refrigerator to keep it from getting taken by someone else. The hospital had become so familiar that he actually had a favorite table in the small kitchen area.

He set down his red sketchbook and arranged the soda and crackers so he could mind-map some ideas while consuming the snack. He pulled a paper towel off the rack and noticed something written on it.

What looks like an accident could be the start of something wonderful.

As he pulled up his chair, he knocked over the open 20-ounce bottle, which spilled dangerously close to the precious sketchbook and cascaded onto his chair and the floor.

Uttering a curse, he snatched the bottle up as fast as he could. *Dammit! Lost half of it. And that was the last of my cash. No help for it now.* Grabbing some paper towels from above the sink, he sopped up as much as he could, then dialed the ICU nurses' station across the hall. Apologizing, he explained about the mess and asked if they could get housekeeping to send someone with a mop.

At least I saved the sketchbook. Something wonderful, right. As he continued working with the paper towels, Skye came in with a small mop, carrying a bucket.

"Hi, Mr. Roberts!" she said. "Doing a little interior decorating?"

Dan chuckled. "I'm sorry to make more work for you. I'm afraid the older I get, the clumsier I get."

"No problem! I'd have come in here to mop soon, anyway."

"Well, I really appreciate the work you and your colleagues do to keep hospital rooms safe and clean. I know I told you that before, but I suspect you don't get enough recognition."

"Thank you. But I don't want to get in your way. You don't get enough time and space for quiet and relaxation as it is. I'll clean the shower while you're finishing up."

"Please, let me just step over to the counter. I don't want to get in *your* way."

"That sounds familiar," she said with a smile. Dan cocked his head in curiosity. "Oh, it's like we've had this conversation before. You said pretty much the same thing in your daughter's room the other day."

"Speaking of that," Dan said. "I wanted to ask you about something."

Skye felt her chest tighten a little. "What's that?"

"Hope has been here a lot in her 20 years, somewhere between 35 and 40 times, a half dozen times in the ICU. We've always appreciated the folks who clean the rooms and the whole hospital, but we've never seen any spend significant time inside a room. They're friendly enough, but they get in and out. You... you actually talk with us when you're in there. I've noticed you looking at Hope, almost like you're listening. It's just a bit... unusual. Do you have a disabled brother or sister or something else that makes you particularly interested in kids like Hope?"

"No, nothing like that, although when I was 10 or 11 I spent a couple of months here myself. Maybe I have a little more empathy for the situation here."

"That makes sense. It's just that we're kind of protective of Hope, you know, she can't look out for herself or tell us if anyone took advantage of her or anything like that, so I get a little antsy if someone maybe shows what could be an unhealthy interest in her."

Dan paused, waiting for a response, watching. Skye said nothing.

"It's just that one nurse mentioned something about you spending time in Hope's room when we aren't around."

Awkward silence. Then Skye said, "Is that a problem?"

Dan looked at his feet, hands in pocket. "Honestly, I'm not sure. Grace noticed and said something to me about it. I think she's nervous about it, and when she gets nervous, I get nervous."

He looked up at her. "But I can tell that she seems calmer after you've been in her room. She definitely responds better to some people than to others. We have one nurse at home that just stresses her out, apparently by existing. Any idea why she might particularly like you?"

Skye took a spray bottle and cloth to the kitchen counter and began cleaning, talking as she cleaned to hide her discomfort. "I don't know, maybe I'm just sympathetic, having been a patient here and all. Um, I guess it could be because, well, uh, I passed on a hint to Erica that they might want to check out her stomach, her abdomen."

"That came from you? How did you know they needed to check that?" Dan suddenly looked very serious. "You didn't *examine* her or anything, did you?"

"No, no, not at all! I just sorta kinda had a feeling, is all, and so I thought I should say something. Just instinct, I guess, or maybe a lucky guess."

Dan looked perplexed. "Well. I'm glad that you said something, glad you had that *instinct* or whatever it was. But... I don't know, Skye. I'm really uncomfortable about this."

"You're not the only one," Skye said under her breath, then worried that Dan might have heard. Dan stood silent for long moments, then said, "I appreciate what you've done for her, don't get me wrong. But this is, to say the least, highly unusual. I... I may have to say something to someone about this."

Skye felt as if her insides wanted to exit through her head. *Shit! I really need this job!* "I'm sorry if I overstepped! I just wanted to help!"

"I don't doubt that, but you have to agree it looks a little odd."

She turned to face him. "I don't want to cause trouble. And I don't want to *be* in trouble. What if I make sure I don't go into her room?"

"Then how is her room going to get cleaned?"

"I'll just ask to get transferred to one of the regular floors. Someone else can come up to the ICU. You won't have to worry about it anymore. Just, please, don't say anything to anyone! I really need this job, and I'm still new at it, still on probation."

Dan ran his hand through his hair, looking down. "I don't know. I mean, you've obviously been good for Hope. But if anything happens, and it turns out someone not family, not a medical professional, had something to do with her care... we could *all* be in a lot of trouble. And Grace... I really don't need Grace amped up. She worries enough already."

"I'll put in for a transfer right now. They can have someone else up here by tomorrow, and I've already cleaned your room for today, so I won't have to go in there at all." She backed out of the little kitchen as she talked. When she reached the door to the hall, she turned and practically ran out, leaving her mop and cleaning equipment behind and Dan standing there, shaking his head.

He saw a spot on the table that Skye missed in her haste. He pulled a rag from her cart to wipe it up, and an old-fashioned pink telephone message slip fell out. The message in the same handwriting as that on the paper towel said, "Fear can blind you. Look again."

Dan felt the hair rise on his neck, muttered, "Can't be." He stepped quickly to the door and looked up and down the hallway, but he was all alone.

Chapter Four

Everything Changes

S kye collapsed on her bed. *For real, the Skye is falling,* she thought. She acknowledged to herself what she was sure everyone else could tell: she was exhausted.

Some of it came from the workload. Housecleaning (*environmental technology,* she reminded herself) involved a heavy load in the ICU, but the fourth floor had a lot more rooms with a lot more routine cleaning. The nurses were friendly enough, but there were so many more, and none seemed inclined to engage in conversation on infrequent breaks. Each day became a blur of mopping, surface cleaning, emptying trash room after room after room.

But she knew much of her exhaustion had little to do with the amount of work she had. She thought back to her visit with Irene that afternoon. It started with Irene's inquiry about the previous week.

"So, have you had any more interactions with Hope?"

"Not with Hope. I did interact with another child in the ICU."

"Oh, how did that go?"

"It was like with Hope, though Charlie's situation is different. He is in a coma because of an accident, so he was confused."

"Tell me what happened."

Her phone chimed, even though she had set it for Do Not Disturb. She glanced at it and saw it was her mother asking about the job. She clicked one of the pre-programmed responses for "in a meeting" and kept talking.

Skye detailed the conversation Monday morning with Charlie and Erica, ending with, "I felt really good about it, but then the next thing I know, it all sort of came crashing down."

Irene tilted her head to the side and pursed her lips. "Crashing down?"

Skye sighed and told Irene about her conversation with Dan on Monday afternoon. "After that, I went straight down to the scheduler and got moved to the fourth floor. I started there on Tuesday, and I've been working there ever since."

Irene sat in silence for a few moments, then sighed heavily. "I can feel your disappointment, I think. I hate to be stereotypical, but... how does that make you feel?"

"Like I'm giving in. Giving in to economic pressure or something. I mean, I really need this job, but I always swore I'd never diminish myself to fit a corporate mold. That's not what this is, but it feels that way."

She looked out the window behind Irene. Irene waited patiently in silence.

"The job *does* matter to me. I want to do a good job, but it has gone from being a sort of mission to being just a job, just a way to get money for living and for school. I think I've let fear into the driver's seat somehow."

"That will wear you out, although you don't need to beat yourself up for deciding to remain safe, to take care of yourself."

"But there's taking care of myself, and then there's taking *care* of myself! It feels like in order to feed my body, so to speak, I have to neglect my soul. I don't even know what that means. Not knowing exhausts me! I just wish someone could tell me what to do."

Irene smiled. "You're not alone in that sentiment. Ironically enough, that feeling may be one of the most common, but the feeling often is some flavor of 'I feel completely alone.'"

Skye nodded. "That's it exactly. So, it *does* sort of help that I'm not alone in feeling alone. Weird."

They both chuckled, and Irene said, "I'm not telling you to take chances with your job, but I *do* think you need to give some thought to how to, as you say, feed your soul as well as your body. It doesn't have to be either-or. Look for a way to be both-and."

Skye nodded again. "OK, I'll work on that. In the meantime, I just have to ignore all this woo-woo stuff. I'll just put my head down and do my job."

"Good luck with that! Any other insights on what you could do to take care of yourself? Spiritually, so to speak?"

Skye looked thoughtful. "I've been meaning to go talk to my pastor about this, get another perspective. I haven't been to church in a long time, but I still feel at home there."

Irene sat up a little straighter. She carefully controlled her expression, but her concern showed. "That could be an excellent idea, especially if it will comfort you. But... I'm sorry, I just have to probe a little. You see, I have sometimes found that church folks can be judgmental about the kinds of experiences you've been having. Sometimes they see legitimate mental health challenges as works of the devil. Not that you are having a mental health challenge beyond stress, but... are you sure it's safe to talk with your pastor about this? Don't get me wrong, they can be truly excellent! I work closely with the chaplains here at the hospital. There are outliers, though, so that's why I'm asking."

"I understand! There are some real crazies out there claiming all sorts of things in the name of Jesus. I even had a friend whose mother told her to be careful hanging around with me, because my dark skin was the Mark of Ham. But Pastor Tim is the real deal, knows his stuff and knows his people."

Irene relaxed and smiled. "I'm glad to hear that. Anything else you could do?"

"It just struck me how long it's been since I visited with Callie at the café. I haven't been there all week! I miss the coffee, and I miss talking with Callie. It may not seem like a huge deal, but that's a really simple way for me to chill a bit, treat myself, you know?"

"I think you should do that! I've often said that coffee is proof that God loves us and wants us to be happy, not beer."

"Plus, nobody will ever card me over a cup of coffee."

"That's true! You know, I've been to that café many times, but I've never seen Callie there. I need to meet her sometime and thank her for referring you to me."

"I think she works Monday. I will make time to get over there, and if you come by during my break time, I'll introduce you."

"Thanks! I'll look forward to it!"

Now, she wasn't sure about introducing Irene to Callie at all. The blow-up with Hope's family left her questioning everything she had experienced, whether it was a blessing or a curse, even if it *was* real. Even working on the fourth floor hadn't freed her from her "visions," if she could call them that. She hadn't even told Irene about her experience that morning. She had come out of the staff elevator just as a couple of nurses brought an unconscious boy onto it, headed for the surgical floor. It was obvious the boy was missing a leg, though probably not recently since he showed no evidence of trauma, just a flat sheet where his leg should have been.

But Skye could also see a misty version of the boy floating over the bed as they wheeled him into the elevator, a version with both legs intact. When he saw Skye looking right at him, he smiled and waved as the elevator doors closed.

Skye didn't know if she wanted to introduce Callie to Irene, even though Callie had connected them in the first place. She knew Irene would keep confidentiality, but still—what if Callie picked up on just exactly how weird Skye had become?

I just know I'm exhausted, she thought. *I don't know if I can handle seeing floating kids. Guess I should talk with Irene about that.*

***

Erica was trying to put a new IV in for Hope when Dan and Grace arrived Monday morning. Hope lay still, showing no discomfort as Erica sought a vein not overly scarred, strong enough to sustain yet one more insertion. All the usual sites had long lost their viability for IVs, so every time one infiltrated or otherwise blew, it grew harder to find a viable site.

"Your work is certainly cut out for you," Grace said.

"I know. I hate to keep probing, but we absolutely must get a line going. I know she doesn't react, but I hate to think that I'm hurting her."

Erica took a step back, ran the back of her wrist across her forehead.

"I'll bet doing that over and over all day can be hard on your back," Dan said.

"It sure can, although we can raise the bed easily. Still, the harder thing is when I have to hurt a kid to take care of her. I don't know which is worse—when they scream like someone's killing them and it takes two of us plus a parent to hold them down, or when you can't tell if they're hurting. I try to watch the pulse monitor on Hope, and if it goes up, I figure there's a problem. But it's hard to tell."

She sighed, and then said mostly to herself, "I wish Skye were here."

Dan perked up. "Skye?"

Grace said, "Isn't she the young lady who keeps the room so neat and clean?"

"Yes, she is. Sorry, I was just thinking out loud. She does a great job with the rooms."

"So, why were you wishing for her?" Dan asked. "Someone else cleaned the room earlier."

"Now that you mention it," Grace said, "We haven't seen her all week. She was always so friendly!"

"It's just that Skye really has a way with kids, especially sick kids. She may be cleaning staff right now, but I think she has a real future, maybe as a nurse or a doctor or a counselor. She doesn't get out of her lane, but... well, she has picked up on some things with several kids here and alerted us. It's always handy to have as many eyes on these kids as possible, and she's been really helpful."

"Helpful in what way? Beyond keeping the room clean, I mean."

"I guess you could say that she tends to, I don't know, *sense* things? I mean... like, she was the one who suggested to me that we might want to check out that lower abdominal thing. I said something to Dr. Powell, and he ordered the ultrasound. I think we would have found it eventually, but she gave us an early heads-up. I'm betting it saved Hope days of discomfort."

"Yeah, I had heard something about her involvement with that."

Grace looked at Dan, puzzled. He had not told her about his conversation with Skye the previous week, or that he might know why she hadn't been around this week.

"And then there was a boy who had an ATV accident last week who was unconscious for several days." Erica paused, remembering, choosing her words carefully. "I can't talk about another case, but I can tell you Skye was a comfort to him and a help to me. Maybe it's because she was a patient here herself at one point, unconscious for a long time."

Dan raised his eyebrows. "She was?"

"Yes. Privacy, and all that, I can't go into detail, but she's open about it. She got struck by lightning or something when she was a kid, spent weeks here. She even volunteered here with Child Life so she could help with kids like her. So I think she really connects with sick kids in a special way.

"Anyway, I do pretty well at 'reading' kids, what they're feeling, how they're doing, but I would just feel better if she gave me some idea whether I was hurting Hope too much trying to get this IV started."

Dan nodded quietly, looking down. "Do you think her ability to connect with some kids might go pretty deeply?"

"What do you mean?"

"I'm not sure. Like, she's so empathetic that she can sort of intuit some things about them that nobody has told her?"

"I've heard of people like that," Grace said. "It's almost like they're psychic or something. Is that what you're thinking? Maybe Skye has that kind of connection to sick kids? Our daughter in particular?"

After a few moments, he said, "I feel the need for some caffeine. Good luck with the IV!" He squeezed Hope's ankle, kissed Grace quickly, and left.

I have to think about this. And coffee helps me think. I hope I can beat the lunch bunch.

***

The demands of work on the fourth floor made it hard to get away for much of a break, but after Skye's conversation with Irene last Friday, she decided she really needed to make the time for a visit to the café. Even though it had been over a week since her last visit, when she walked in, Callie had already begun setting "their" table.

"Wow! It's almost like you were expecting me," Skye said. "I feel so honored!"

"I know, right?" Callie said. "I just about know when to start the coffee, even before you get here."

She set a steaming cup in front of Skye, a white porcelain mug instead of the standard issue paper cups. "You get to use one of my personal favorites," Callie said as she settled in across the table. "You must have been really busy. So, had any interesting conversations with patients lately?"

"Oddly enough, yes, and with more than just Hope. You wouldn't believe all that has happened in the last week!"

"You might be surprised what I would believe. Tell me what's been going on."

"Let's see…. Last Monday morning, Erica asked if I would look in on room 511. She said, 'They need their trash emptied, but I think maybe that boy could use a visit with you, if you know what I mean.' He was confused, didn't know where he was. He'd been in a ATV accident, and it was like with Hope all over again, his body lying still in the bed and him, his spirit or whatever it is, sitting up and looking all around. He said he'd been trying to talk to people and nobody would talk back to him.

"I told him as best I could what was going on. I think he's about 13, close to the age I was when I spent time in the ICU. I didn't want to freak him out, but I told him I could see and hear him when other people couldn't. He asked if he was dead! He calmed down when I told him that, no, he was just unconscious, and he probably wouldn't even remember this. But I told him I'd ask Erica to explain to him what happened."

"Wow! That must have really helped him!"

"I think so. And I think it means something that Erica would even ask me to go in there. In fact, I went out to the desk and got Erica back in there. She talked to him, and he had some questions that I relayed, and she answered them. She looked a little freaked out. She said, 'I shouldn't be doing this with you here, privacy and all that.' And I said, 'He says it's OK. Of course, you just have to take my word for it.' She laughed a little nervously, but she kept going, and when we finished, he lay back down in his body and his pulse calmed way down."

"Let me play counselor here. How did that make you feel?"

"Funny you should say that? I'm not sure a real counselor has ever asked me that directly until recently, but Irene did just last Friday. But that's what it all comes down to anyway, isn't it? So, here's the honest answer: when it was happening, it felt so right! I guess I mean, fulfilling. But when it was over? I had to deal with the part of me going, 'What the heck are you doing? This is nuts! You're going to get in trouble!' So I was both elated and scared."

A shadow flitted across Skye's face. "Things really changed that afternoon, though. It turns out word got to Hope's dad that I had spent a lot of time in Hope's room. They're very protective of her, of course, and I think they worried whether I had some unsavory reason for going in her room when they weren't there. I just wanted to give Hope a chance to talk, but they didn't know that, of course. Dad hinted that he might have to talk to my supervisor, and that freaked me out. I asked for a transfer to another unit, and they put me on the fourth floor."

"Wow! I'll bet that hurt a lot!"

"In more ways than one! I don't mind the extra work. I just don't feel the connection with the nurses, and I'm not helping any kids, not like Hope and Charlie. I kept worrying that I would get in trouble, and I don't even know if Hope is still in the hospital or how she's doing. She may have been moved to the second floor, or sent home, and Hope may think I just disappeared."

"For whatever it's worth, I do see Dan... I mean, Mr. Roberts down here still, every couple of days."

"Has he said anything about Hope?"

"I haven't actually had a chance to talk with him. I've seen him, but I don't think he's seen me."

Callie smiled to herself, stirred her still steaming coffee. "If you don't mind me asking, how are things going with Irene? Is that helping?"

Skye sat facing the entrance to the café, so she could see that at that very moment, Irene came through the door.

"Speak of the devil! Here she comes now." Skye waved, and Irene waved back and started over to the table. Callie, however, didn't turn.

"Hey, Skye, time for a coffee refresher, right?"

"That, and conversation. I look forward to visiting with Callie as much as I look forward to the coffee."

"Excellent! I've heard so much about her. I'd love to meet her."

"She's right here! Irene, Callie. Callie, Irene."

Callie sat still. Irene looked around, next table, behind her, then back at Skye with raised eyebrows. "Who are you talking to?"

Skye pushed her chair back slowly, looking from Irene to Callie, raising her hands. "Oooooh, no, don't do this! Callie is sitting right there. Don't tell me you're not seeing her!"

Irene looked right at Callie, it seemed, but turned back to Skye and gently said, "I have to tell you I don't see anyone there."

"Don't freak out," Callie said. "It's not what you're thinking."

"Don't freak out," Irene said. "May I sit down?"

Skye continued to stare at Callie, but said to Irene, "Sure, help yourself, if you don't mind sitting with a crazy woman."

Irene sat in the third seat, making a sort of triangle around the table. She slowly reached out and took Skye's hand.

"Skye, I have a confession. There's a reason I'm taking a special interest in you and your... situation. Let me put it this way. Just because I don't see anyone there doesn't mean there's no one there. You're not crazy. In fact, I can sense that, without a doubt in my mind, there really is someone there. I can sense it, even though I see nothing."

Callie looked steadily at Skye, smiling slightly, saying nothing. "What do you mean?" Skye asked. "Sense? See?"

Callie said, "You need to have this conversation right now. I don't want to distract you, so I will leave you to it. We'll talk again soon."

Skye watched Callie leave through a door labeled "Employees only," while Irene watched Skye. "She's gone, isn't she?" Irene said.

Skye focused on Irene. "Yes, she is. How did you know?"

"If nothing else, I watched you track her as she left. But it also *feels* different, like the chair is truly empty now. That's how it is with me. I don't see people who aren't there. Sometimes I hear them. Most times, I just sense them."

"You keep saying 'sense.' What do you mean? If you don't see them or hear them, how do you sense them?"

"This is as close as I can come to explaining it. Hold out your hand, palm up, about three or four inches above the table. Now, close you eyes, not too tight, but make sure you can't see anything."

Irene held her own hand palm down above Skye's, about an inch away but not touching. She said nothing, but Skye said, "Are you holding your hand over mine?"

"Yes. How did you know?"

"I don't know. Something just felt... I could just feel it. Not like touching-it feeling, but I knew it was there. Maybe I heard something rustle. Maybe I picked up a little heat. I don't know, I just knew."

"That's what it's like for me. I'll just suddenly know someone is present. The first time it happened at a bed-and-breakfast. I was treating myself to a trip after my own recovery from an accident. I choked on a bit of food. Might have died in the restaurant if someone hadn't done that Heimlich maneuver thing on me. The first morning after that, I woke up in my little bedroom and immediately sensed someone else in the room with me. In fact, it felt like someone sat in the high-back chair at the corner of the bed next to the dresser. I could see no one there, but I couldn't shake the feeling."

Irene looked off in the distance, lost in memory.

"I went down to breakfast, and I asked the owner if anyone occupied the room next to mine, thinking maybe I had heard someone over there. When she questioned me, I told her I felt someone else nearby, and she said, 'Oh, that was probably Lola. She's our resident ghost.' That wasn't exactly comforting. She told me guests sometimes saw Lola or heard her moving around in the kitchen. She was the wife of a former owner, and she had died under mysterious circumstances. Priscilla, the new owner, said no one had ever reported anything really bad, and they liked having Lola around since she added 'atmosphere.'

"After that, it kept happening. Around this hospital, a lot of people died over the years, all the way back to the time when the first hospital started here in what had been a residence. The new buildings that have gone up in the last 20 years confuse some of them. Sometimes they talk to me, and I help them move on. I think of it as just another part of my work, although they didn't teach me anything about it when I earned my MSW."

Skye looked as if she might flee at any moment. "So... is Callie... is she dead or something?"

"Well, it's funny. I could certainly sense her presence, but there's something different about her. I didn't hear her say anything, although you seemed to hear her talking. So I'm just going on feel, but somehow the *quality* seemed different. The *size* seemed different, like she had a definite presence in that chair, but also like she filled the entire room. I've never sensed that before."

Skye sat back in her chair, shook her head slowly. "OK, this week has been a little more than I could handle. I have to think about this. Would you excuse me for a bit?"

"By all means. Take your time. It's a lot to process."

Skye pushed back her chair and walked out, her mind spinning. She hardly noticed pushing the button for the elevator, leaving the building, or walking into downtown.

***

As she walked, Skye kept thinking about all the conversations with Callie, how she listened and encouraged, looking for clues that she was something other than what she appeared. *If she's not dead and she's not a patient, who is she? What is she? Will I see her again? Do I want to see her again? Come to think of it, she referred me to Irene. Is Irene real, or is she another ghost or something? Is any of this real?*

"She's real, Skye, just as real as you."

Skye realized she had walked all the way to the university campus a mile or more away from the hospital, and that she no longer walked alone. Looking to her right, she saw Callie, familiar Callie, walking alongside.

They walked in silence for a bit. Finally, Skye said, "You know, I'm surprised to see you and not surprised, all at the same time. It's like that line from that cheesy Nicholas Cage movie, *Con Air*, where he looks out the back of the airplane and they're dragging a sports car behind them through the air, and he says, 'On any other day, that might seem strange.'"

"Yeah, I know the line you're talking about. I may have let Scott down on that movie."

"What?"

"Never mind. In any case, you weren't supposed to find out that I was anything other than a barista, at least not this early. I couldn't just leave you wandering around the city trying to sort things out. So I thought I should come visit you a little more."

Skye stopped dead in her tracks. "Who the hell are you, anyway?"

"Before I answer that, we probably should keep walking. And you might want to put earbuds in."

"Why?"

"I think you're a little concerned that people might think you're crazy, right? If they see you standing here talking to yourself, they might think that. But if you're walking with earbuds in, they'll think you're talking on your phone."

Skye noticed a couple of passing college students looking at her sideways. "I don't have any earbuds with me."

Callie sighed and handed Skye a pair of shiny black bluetooth earbuds. "Were you just holding those?" Skye said. "I didn't see you reach into your pocket or anything."

"First thing, Skye, you don't want to try too hard to figure out how all this works. But there *are* a few things that we probably need to get straight. So, if it's OK with you, let's just walk and talk a bit. Remember that you're the only one seeing me, though."

Skye started walking, putting the earbuds in as she moved. Finally, she said, "Just tell me this. Was the coffee real, or did I imagine drinking it?"

Callie smiled, then burst out laughing, and after a moment, Skye joined in. She laughed so hard that she had to sit down on a low concrete wall around one of the stately campus buildings. When she recovered, she sighed and said, "That felt good. I guess everything built until the absurdity of it all came to a head. But seriously, was the coffee real?"

"It was. And wasn't it the best coffee ever?"

"Oh, yeah. That's what made me doubt its reality. OK, so back to the last question: who the hell are you?"

"It's complicated. Let me see if I can put it into a context that will make sense. You have heard creative people, writers and artists, talk about being moved by their muse?"

"Yeah, sure. I had an uncle who worked at a newspaper, and he used to make fun of what he viewed as sensitive artistic types who 'had to wait for their muse.' He said he had to get a story turned in by 3 PM whether or not he felt inspired."

"That's certainly true. But there is such a thing as a muse. The ancient Greeks actually identified nine Muses, each having responsibility for certain kinds of creativity. The Romans had a similar understanding. They didn't say someone *was* a genius. They said someone *had* a genius, sort of like having a guiding spirit or messenger. Just about every ancient culture came up with similar concepts, even though they didn't interact with each other. Each culture had their own names for the same idea.

"When different cultures come up with the same concepts, it's a good sign of some underlying reality that they all sense in common. They may not understand it, but they sense it, and they come up with stories to explain what they sense."

Callie took a deep breath, then went on. "I'm the one the ancient Greeks called Calliope. My eight sisters and I help humans with their creativity. It really is what makes humans human—creativity. But we don't whisper ideas to you or anything like that. We reflect *with* you, helping you bring out your natural creativity. Most people never notice our presence at all."

Callie looked down as she walked, and a sadness came over her. "Some people don't recognize their own creativity. Because they don't draw or play music or something like that, they convince themselves they're not creative. We grieve when that happens, because they miss a big part of themselves that way."

She looked up and smiled. "Others reach down inside themselves and discover a spark. We don't light that spark, you understand. But we help people fan the flame. Some hear us more than see us. Some see us in different forms and different ways. In a lot of ways, we are a product of your imagination, so when you ask if I'm real, I have to honestly say that, in some ways, I'm imaginary.

"But I'm not imaginary the way your invisible friend was imaginary when you were seven years old. Tisha, I think was her name, right?"

"How do you know about Tisha?"

"Hello! What have I been telling you about creativity? She came from your creativity, totally made up by you. I transcend you, helping lots of people across eons of time, across cultures. So I was there with you when you were making up Tisha, even though you didn't know I was there."

"This just leads me to dozens of other questions. Like, if you have always been with me, why am I *seeing* you now? Why didn't you just stay in the background? And why do those sensitive creative types think you desert them? And why am I seeing you as Greek? Why aren't I seeing some African deity? And, I don't know, I think I may need to go talk to my pastor, because I don't know of *anything* in my religion that goes along with this. Maybe you're the devil in disguise!"

"That's a lot. It's probably more than what we have time to go into, and really, it's more than you need to know. I'm not trying to hide anything from you. But my job isn't to explain the structure of reality to you. It's to help you draw out your creativity. Did you fix yourself some food in the microwave yesterday after work?"

"Sure. I made a baked potato, and then fixed up a frozen chicken pot pie later."

"Do you understand exactly how a microwave oven works? Or do you just know what buttons to push?"

"For all I know, there are squirrels in there with little hot plates," Skye said, shrugging her shoulders. "OK, I get it. I don't have to understand it all. But, Callie... Calliope... whatever I am supposed to call you... if I'm going to convince myself I'm not crazy, I need to know a little about what's happening with me. Let's start with why you're here right now."

"Let's walk again."

They began moving again, angling toward old downtown.

"So, first, I don't know all there is to know. I'm not a deity the way you may think of such, although it's hard to put me in a familiar classification. That matters because you may think I have everything planned out, and that I know what's going to happen ahead of time; but I don't. Although I do experience time differently from you, I cannot 'tell the future' as you might call it. So I have to admit that it took me by surprise when Irene came into the coffee shop.

"As I said, most of the time, a human doesn't even know one of us is around. If they interact with one of us, they may think we're a chance acquaintance, or someone they see regularly in a particular context—like a barista or a hairdresser. It never occurs to them that in a small town or neighborhood, you would expect to run into your hairdresser at the grocery store. If you never see someone except in one particular place, that could be one of us.

"But sometimes, we need to get a little more direct. Sometimes, one of us will get 'outed,' like today. Sometimes, one of our 'clients' will figure out what we were doing after the fact. Take Dan Roberts, for instance."

Skye glanced sideways at Callie as they walked. "Dan Roberts? Hope's dad?"

"The same. I worked with him, mostly listening but sometimes leaving him notes. He didn't need creative help so much as he needed reminding of what was most important to him. After leaving his conscious awareness, I left him a note to help him continue on his path. But I didn't need to stay 'forward.' Had I done so, it might have actually interfered with his work."

Callie smiled to herself, remembering.

"Since I don't experience time the way you do, in a way I'm with Dan right now, as well as countless others. But in your way of dealing with time, everything has a beginning, and everything has an ending. How things will play out in any given timeline remains uncertain until you have made particular observations, taken particular actions. It's a bit tricky to explain, which is why I think it's important for you to understand you don't have to understand it all. You can't, Skye. *I* can't. I just know what I need to do at any point where I cross into your world, the world of anyone I'm helping.

"And what I needed to do with you, *for* you, after Irene walked into the picture, was to drop the facade."

"I have about a million more questions now, but.... OK, I still don't know exactly why you are here with *me*. You're talking about writers and artists..."

"...and philosophers and astronomers and cooks and plumbers..."

"OK, all those people, but I don't do that. I'm just a fancy cleaning woman."

"A fancy cleaning woman who has an amazing ability to connect people who otherwise could not connect."

"That needs a muse?"

"That doesn't *need* a muse. You *have* a muse. And what I'm doing with you, for you, right now isn't putting ideas in your head, or telling you how to write, or planting suggestions about how to plan that plumbing system. I'm here for one thing, and one thing only: to help you believe in yourself. Only then can you bring out the creative being that is your core.

"You wrestle with whether or not I'm real, but the more important question is whether you recognize that *you* are real. That's what we're dealing with right now."

They reached the main road through downtown, turning toward the river. Skye looked off toward the horizon. "I don't know what's real right now. It wouldn't surprise me to wake up any minute and find I've dreamed all this. Maybe I'm even dreaming *me*."

"That's always an interesting question. But I need to tell you this: things are about to get really *real*. If you doubt yourself now, you will face circumstances that will make you doubt yourself even more. So if you remember nothing else, remember this: who you are and *what* you are is enough."

They had just reached the bridge crossing the river with four lanes of traffic whizzing by a couple of feet away. A passing pickup truck almost clipped Skye with his outsized mirrors, and she could feel the *whoosh* as it went by. She turned to look behind them for any others and moved closer to the railing. When she looked around to see if she crowded Callie, she found herself alone.

***

Dan missed his regular visits to The Blissful Bean back home while Hope was in the hospital. But he appreciated having the little café where he could get coffee almost as good. It served much the same function as The BB—a place to get away, to get quiet, to think. Maybe even write a little.

Today, though, he only wrote in his red sketchbook, his "thinking tool." Over a cup of coffee with lots of artificial sweetener and cream, he doodled in a corner of an empty page and then jotted some thoughts into a mind map. After a few minutes, he tore out the page, examined the map as a whole, and then started listing bullet points from the map to give some order to his thoughts.

- Skye could not have known what she knows without some connection to Hope.

- Scam? Will she try to leverage this?

- Could a nurse have divulged private information?

- What if this is real?

- How will this change things?

- Should we try to get Skye to come back? What happens if Skye bails?

I really need my laptop, Dan thought. *It would be so much easier to arrange this.*

"You don't need a laptop, Dan. You just need your heart, and you have that deeply."

For a moment, Dan froze, not daring to look up. When he did, sitting across from him sat Callie. She wore a hospital food services uniform instead of her more casual Blissful Bean attire, and her hair looked different, but he instantly recognized his Muse. His eyes misted, and for another moment he couldn't speak.

"It's good to see you, too, Dan. I would ask how the writing is going, but I already know." She smiled warmly and handed him a fresh cup of coffee, just like he remembered.

Finally, he said, "I am very glad to see you, and very surprised! I know how you use your magic beans to help people create, but I wouldn't think a hospital café would be the best place to do that. Am I about to be blocked or something that I would need your help again?"

Callie leaned across the table and put her hand on Dan's wrist. "You don't need my help. You're doing fine. It was you all along, anyway. I'm not here for you. I'm here for someone else."

Dan looked around, but no one else in the café paid them any attention. "There's another writer here?"

Callie laughed. "Writers aren't the only creative people, you know."

"Oh, I know! I know how much you helped Grace with her graphic arts. Maybe a nurse secretly paints on the side? And given their challenges, medical folks certainly get creative! But... if you're not here for me, why are we having this conversation? As glad as I am to see you, I have to ask why."

"That doesn't surprise me. As I recall, you've done well asking *why*, and you helped a lot of other people with that. I'm talking with you right now because you can help someone else use their creativity in ways that you have probably never considered before. You know my methods, so it won't surprise you that I have a question or two for you."

"I'm ready. Shoot."

"If I had told you who I really was when we first met, would you have believed me?"

Without hesitation, Dan said, "Absolutely not. I would have thought you were crazy. I would have wondered how you planned to scam me."

"So it took some experience before you were open to, shall we say, a more direct conversation?"

"That's putting it mildly. You made me doubt my sanity, and that's something Grace already doubted."

"But Grace eventually believed you, right?"

"After that note you left for her, yes. I don't know what was in it. She's never shared it, and I respect her privacy too much to ask.

But after I took the envelope to her, she read it, looked at me, and said, 'OK. She's real. Don't ask me how I know, but I know.'"

"And I won't break that privacy now. She just needed her own experience. I only mention it to ask this: how much difference did it make to you that she believed you as well as believed *in* you?"

Dan pondered for a moment. He looked up, his eyes once again moist. "It meant the world to me."

"So, now: do you know someone at this moment who may doubt her own sanity, who could use someone to believe in her?"

Skye. Skye needs to hear this from me.

"I see you know who I'm talking about. Here's one more thought: you knew deep down what you were put on this earth for. You just needed a little nudge to help you remember what you already knew. She, on the other hand, is doubting who she is at her core, thinking maybe she is simply *wrong*, not holding a wrong opinion or working the wrong job. *Wrong.* It's hard to live with yourself when you think that way, much less achieve your creative potential. There's believing. And there's believing *in*."

Once again, Callie reached across and squeezed Dan's wrist. "Gotta go. Revealing myself so explicitly is getting to be too much of a habit. As glad as I am to see you, I would really rather have done it the 'old-fashioned way,' influences and nudges, and all that."

"So, what made you change your usual approach?"

"Let's just say things have become much more urgent. My sisters may be upset with me, and Dad is really ticked. So don't make me regret this. Now, excuse me. I have coffee to sling."

Dan opened his sketchbook and wrote:

There's believing. And there's believing *in*.

When he looked up, Callie had vanished.

Chapter Five

Rescue

I t was only 9 PM, but Skye had already huddled in bed with her favorite comforter and stuffed animals from her childhood gathered around. The day had overwhelmed her, and her parents would come home Wednesday unless their plans changed. She needed the solitude and quiet for processing and self-care. With a cup of hot chocolate on the nightstand, propped up in a mound of pillows with a new Stephen King book, she intended to immerse herself in a world where she didn't have to think about her unanswered questions.

That's probably why she fell asleep early.

Almost as soon as her eyes closed and her breathing settled into a slow, steady rhythm, she began dreaming. That wasn't unusual. What *was* unusual was that she *knew* she was in a dream.

She flew down Main Street, away from the hospital, just at the level of the telephone wires. It *felt* like she flew, and she could look down on the street, but she moved as if she were swimming through the air. Dog paddling, in fact. She could go up or down depending on how she inclined her body, although if she paddled too slowly, she lost altitude. Still, staying aloft took little effort as she flew above the curiously empty street.

Maybe I can see the backyards of some of these fancy houses. The telephone wires kept her confined to the street, but if she nosed higher, she could get over them. Just as she turned to explore behind a big Victorian, she realized she had company.

She looked to her right and saw Hope flying beside her, appearing to pilot a hospital bed. IV lines strung to the corners like reins with which she steered, like a mattress version of Pegasus. Hope gathered both lines into one hand, then smiled and waved. Skye waved back, momentarily causing her to dip in her flight before she started dog paddling again.

"Fancy seeing you here!" Skye shouted.

"Yes! Looks like this is the only way to see you, though, since you haven't been around the hospital!"

"I'm at the hospital. I'm just on a different floor."

"I missed you! Why did you leave?" Hope threw her weight to one side and the hospital bed rotated a full turn around its horizontal axis. "Wheeeee!" Her hospital gown billowed in the wind, her waist-length hair streaming behind her like a flag.

"I transferred because I made your dad nervous. I was afraid he would report me and I would get in trouble."

"That poopy-head!"

"He's just trying to protect you, Hope. He doesn't know me, and he doesn't know we can talk."

Hope snorted. "He may be trying to protect me, but if he sent you away, he may have killed me."

"Killed you?!? What do you mean?"

The dream scene instantly shifted. They stood on a dry, cracked desert like pictures Skye had seen of Death Valley. A scraggly cactus struggled to survive next to them, the sun impossibly bright. From the sky, as if the whole world became a giant speaker, the first five notes from the theme song of "The Good, the Bad, and The Ugly" played once.

"There's something going on with my lungs. I don't think the nurse can tell, because that thing that monitors my oxygen is not going off. Maybe it's bugged. I don't know. I just know that I'm slowly drowning. That's why I'm here right now. Daddy says **I go to sleep** when there is something going on I don't like, and he's right.

I'm having fun flying my bed around, because I don't know how much longer I can do this. And I don't know what happens when I die. Maybe I'll just never have to go back to my body. Maybe I'll disappear, like turning off a light. I don't know. So I'm flying around while I can.

"If you had been around the ICU, I could have told you a couple of days ago. Since I don't know how much longer I have, I thought I might find you here. At least I could say goodbye."

Skye sat bolt upright in her bed, knocking the dregs of hot chocolate off the nightstand. She looked at the clock. Midnight.

"I have *got* to get to the hospital!" she said out loud to no one, and scrambled to get clothes on and out to her car, remembering to grab her employee badge on the way out.

She reached the hospital far faster than usual. At midnight she didn't have to deal with rush hour traffic, plus she felt great urgency. On the way, she debated how she could get the night shift nurses in the ICU to take her seriously. As she neared the hospital, she slowed down, not wanting to attract attention.

The last thing I need is to get pulled over, she thought.

She parked on the street close to the employees' entrance. She could hear music coming from some bars two streets over, closer to the university, but the area around the hospital had hardly any cars or traffic, a stark contrast to the density of traffic during the day. She slung the backpack over her shoulder and walked as confidently as she could to the staff entrance. The door opened easily to her badge.

She felt like a thief breaking in. *I'm definitely out of my lane.* Then she heard another voice in her head, felt more than heard, reminding her that people in a hospital uniform with an employee's badge could go almost anywhere in the hospital without a question, and nobody much noticed the cleaning crew. She went to her locker and quickly pulled on a spare uniform, then picked up a bucket, some rags, and a bottle of spray cleaner.

The elevator doors opened on the fifth floor, where Jimmy practically ran over her with a ride-on scrubber. He stopped short, inches away. "Whoa! You gotta be careful getting off the elevator in the middle of the night, Skye! What are you even doing here now? You should have gone home hours ago."

Skye caught her breath. "I'm sorry, Jimmy! I, uh, I came in for some overtime. The ICU needed a little extra clean-up, so here I am."

"Phyllis needed help? Man, there must be a real mess in there. Good luck!"

Skye stepped out of his path, and Jimmy continued his route around the floor. She tried to appear casual as she headed to the back entrance to the ICU. She opened it to find Phyllis just on the other side, sorting bags of laundry.

"What are you doing here? Are you late, or are you early? I thought you were on another floor, anyway."

Skye looked sheepish. "I'm not really here for work. Can you do me a favor and not tell anyone I was here?"

"You here for a *personal* visit? You know you ain't supposed to be doing that."

"I know, I know, but this is *really* important. Please don't turn me in! I just need to do something real quick for a friend."

Phyllis regarded her skeptically, shook her head, grabbed two bags in each hand, and began dragging them toward the service elevator.

"I ain't seen nothing," she said. "If you'd have been 5 minutes slower, I would've been gone, and that's exactly what I'm gonna be. Just watch out. Brenda's on the floor, and I have a feeling I know who you're doing something for. Brenda don't put up with no nonsense. She can get you fired out of here faster than blueberries through a goose. Just be careful."

***

Do I really want to do this? Brenda had a reputation for doing everything by the book, military-like, and for expecting her nurses to do so as well. As a nursing night shift supervisor, Brenda never crossed paths with Skye, but Skye didn't want to tangle with her. She slipped her badge into a pocket, hoping that if someone spotted her, she could at least remain somewhat anonymous.

Skye peaked through the partially opened door. She could see straight to Hope's room, and two or three nurses sitting at computer stations outside rooms in between. *Act like you belong.* She remembered that bit of advice from an instructor in a journalism class who talked about how to reach difficult sources. *I'll bet that works in a lot of other places.* She grabbed a couple of empty trash bags and walked out of the back area into the main ICU, acting much more confident than she felt.

Five steps. Ten steps. Nobody looked up. She glanced to her left, trying to look casual. Brenda sat at a desktop computer, glued to the monitor, watching a training video. The floor doc sat nearby, engrossed in a lab report. She walked straight to Hope's room without challenge, entered, and closed the door behind her.

"It's about time," translucent Hope said. "I had almost given up on you."

"I got here as quick as I could. This isn't like popping up here on my lunch break or something."

"I'm glad you're here. I don't think I have a lot of time. I can feel my heart working too hard."

"What do you want me to do?"

"I think you'd better get my nurse in here. It's Tammy tonight."

Skye hesitated. "I really don't want to push the button. I'd rather do it sort of unofficially. What's Tammy look like?"

"Short, blond hair, kinda frizzy. It makes her look a little like a dandelion, especially since she has dark skin like you. And she's tall, really tall."

"That should be easy enough to spot."

Skye went to the exterior door and opened it a crack. Close to the front entrance of the unit behind the desk, she immediately spotted Tammy intent on typing something into a computer. Skye walked casually around the desk as if leaving the unit, but stopped and turned before exiting to face Tammy, and waited.

Tammy looked up but kept typing. "Can I help you with something?"

"I hope so. Hope Roberts in 509 is having a medical emergency that is hard to spot, and I need for you to come check her out quietly and find it, since I'm not a nurse."

Tammy stopped typing and studied Skye, looking at the Environmental Technician patch on her shoulder.

"Aren't you getting out of your lane a little bit? What makes you think she's having a medical emergency?"

"Look, I know you don't know me, but I have worked here in the ICU before, and I have a ... a connection to Hope. There's not much reason for you to believe me, but I have to try. Please. It's important."

"Who did you say you were?"

She took a deep breath and a deep chance. "My name is Skye Jackson. And I'm not anybody special. I just have a connection to Hope."

"You said that. How did you know I'm Hope's nurse tonight? Were you in her room just now?"

"Yeah, sure, I saw your name on the whiteboard along with the RT and the doctor."

"Funny thing. I was just in there a few minutes ago, and I noticed I hadn't updated the board at shift change. I was going to do that after I checked this lab report, but I haven't done it yet. So I know my name isn't up there. Try again."

"OK. Well, believe it or not... Hope told me."

Tammy crossed her arms and sat back. "Say again?"

"I know. But you have to believe me. Hope told me to come and get you. She needs you."

"Tell me your name again?"

She's getting ready to report me. I should make up a name, she doesn't remember it, I don't have my name tag on, maybe I could get away with it. But... Hope is in danger. She took another deep breath, said, "Skye Jackson."

Tammy sat still for a beat or two, never taking her eyes off Skye. "So, you know Erica, I take it."

Skye perked up. "Yes, I got to know Erica when I worked up here."

"Erica told me that there was someone who had this spooky way of picking up on what goes on with nonverbal kids. Said she hasn't seen you in a week or so. She had Hope today and turned her over to me tonight."

"I don't want to attract a lot of attention. I just want to get Hope some help. And I could be wrong, so I'm hoping you'll check it out. But if I'm right, she needs some attention really quickly."

"Let's go."

Tammy came around the desk and the two of them went into Hope's room, shutting the door behind them.

"So, what's going on?"

"Hope says she feels like she's drowning and her heart is working too hard."

"How do I know that's coming from her? Don't look to me like she's telling anybody anything."

Skye looked at translucent Hope sitting up on the bed with physical Hope lying still underneath her. "Hope, I need something to tell Tammy so she'll know it's you, not me."

"Ask her about her new tattoo. She told somebody about it earlier. Said it used gold ink."

"Hope says to ask you about your new tattoo."

Tammy's eyes widened. "What about it?"

"Hope says it's in gold ink."

"Where is it?"

Skye turned toward Hope. "I don't know," said Hope. "She was talking to Miranda about it. She didn't way where it was, but she said it was her mother's name."

"Hope says she doesn't know. She just heard you talking about it to Miranda. Who's Miranda?"

"That's the respiratory therapist. She was in here earlier, and we were talking about tattoos."

"It had something to do with your mother."

Tammy's eyes misted over. "Yeah, my mom died last year. I got a tattoo of her name right here on the inside of my upper arm earlier today." She pulled up the sleeve of her scrubs to reveal the new tattoo, still covered in plastic wrap. "I haven't showed this to anybody, just talked about it to Miranda. So I guess maybe your girl really is talking to you. Let's see what we can tell."

Tammy started checking the pulse-oximeter more closely. "Hmmm. Her oxygen looks good, but her heart rate is a little erratic, and it's elevated." She took a stethoscope from where it hung on an IV pole and checked each lung quadrant, lingering on the lower right. "I have to admit, this doesn't sound right. Is she hurting?"

"I can't take a deep breath, it just hurts too much," Hope told Skye. "And my legs hurt." Skye passed on the information.

Tammy pondered a moment or two, then said, "Dr. Brandt usually trusts the nurses. I'm going to ask him to order a blood gas, see what's going on there."

"Obviously, I'm not a medical professional, but that makes sense to me." She paused. "I'm not sure why, but if I can make a little suggestion. Since you're going to do a blood gas anyway, you might want to include that test where they check for blood clots."

"A D-dimer? It's a simple test. Might not be a bad idea. What made you think of that if you don't know medicine?"

Skye paused. "I don't really know. Hope didn't tell me. Could just be my Muse, I guess."

"Well, it sort of makes sense. I'll suggest it."

"Thanks, Tammy. I appreciate it."

"I think they should work fast," Hope said.

"Hope says work fast. I'm going to slide out of here. No one needs to know I was here. But... I know this is not the usual way of doing things, but can you just send me a text about what happens?"

Tammy hesitated.

"I'm not asking for detail. I understand patient privacy and I'm not next of kin and all that. Just let me know if Hope's OK. You don't even have to say her name. Please?"

Tammy nodded. "None of this is the usual way. One more won't matter. Sure. Now go on and get out of here before the doctor wonders what's going on. And watch out for Brenda. She's on a rampage tonight."

Skye peaked out the door. Brenda had stepped away from her computer, nowhere to be seen. Skye slipped out and made her way out the back entrance, to the elevator, and out into the night.

***

It had been a long day, even though it had been a short one.

Skye hadn't awakened until 10:30 AM, well past the start of her shift. The midnight run to the ICU along with the increased adrenaline and activity had left her drained, and she slept through her alarm. When she reached the fourth floor, she learned she had been the only one assigned that day, so she had double the work to do in half the time. The entire day had been a scramble. She worked late to get caught up. When she finally left work, she collapsed behind the wheel of her car for a few minutes. *Thank goodness I'll have the house to myself when I get there. I really need the downtime.*

But when Skye pulled in the driveway, her headlights picked up the unexpected sight of her parents' car in the open garage. *I thought they weren't coming home until tomorrow!* She immediately felt a mix of relief and dread. She needed someone to talk with, but she didn't know if she was ready—and, for sure, she would get questioned when she went inside. *Maybe I should go get something to eat first, give them time to get to bed.* At that moment, the front porch light came on and she could see her mother peeking through the curtains. *Too late for that.* She took a deep breath and headed inside.

"Hi, Mom!" she said brightly when she entered the kitchen. "I didn't think you guys would be home until tomorrow! Is everything OK?"

Her mother looked up from unpacking the snack crate they always took on trips. Though they could afford to indulge themselves with "fancy hotel food," as her dad called it, the habits from their early years starting up an accounting firm stuck with them.

"Just because we *can* get that fancy hotel food doesn't mean we *should*," Dad often said, and so they always took plenty of their own snacks on trips.

Mom smiled. "I was going to ask you the same thing. Dad and I decided we had enjoyed about all the leisure time we could stand, and I felt like you had something going on that you weren't telling us about. You've not responded much about the new job, and even ignored some of our texts, which isn't like you. So we decided to save a night in a hotel and come on home. We wanted to surprise you! Here, I brought you something."

Mom walked to their bedroom and came back with something wrapped in brown paper. "We went to the River Arts District yesterday, and I picked this up for you. I didn't have a chance to wrap it properly, but I wanted to give it to you as soon as we got home."

Skye sat down at the kitchen table, peeling away the brown paper and bubble wrap until a twelve-inch-high sculpture of a unicorn revealed itself. Crafted from iridescent white material with subtle flecks of color throughout, the artist had rendered the unicorn's mane and tail as a vibrant rainbow waterfall, with strands of amethyst, turquoise, and sun-kissed gold swaying in an unseen breeze. Its horn—a bright blue accent—added a touch of magic. The sculptor appeared to have caught it in mid-prance with its head held high, as if frozen in a moment of mythical grace.

"It is beautiful, Mom. Thank you."

Mom sat down at the side adjacent to Skye, giving her space while also holding her hand. "When I saw this, I thought immediately of you. Would you like to know why?"

"Yes."

"You have always felt like you were different. When you're a teenager, that's a very uncomfortable feeling. I can remember that feeling. You want more than anything to blend in, to be like your friends, to not be 'the weird one.' I saw that in you more than ever after your run in with the lightning.

"But when you get older, you start to not only get comfortable being different. You start to value what makes you unique. Like this unicorn. When I saw this piece in the artist's shop, I saw that obviously this creature was not a horse. And it didn't want to be a horse. It gloried in being a unicorn. Different. Not for the sake of being different, you understand. A lot of people seek to identify as nonconformists, and in doing so, they simply conform to what other nonconformists do. The unicorn doesn't *try* to be different. It simply is what it is.

"This unicorn has learned that. But it took a while. That's what I saw in this piece, and that's why I had to bring it to you. Do you understand?"

Before she replied, she reached into her backpack and pulled out her notebook. She turned to the next blank page and wrote:

A unicorn doesn't *try* to be different. It simply is what it is.

Skye ran her fingers over the texture of the unicorn's sides, the undulations of the mane and tail, the strength of the body. "I think

I understand. I guess everybody feels weird as teenagers, but I felt like I was weirder than other teenagers. Did you think that of me?"

Mom sat quietly for a moment, time-traveling in her mind. "You don't remember much from the days after you woke up in the hospital, after the lightning struck you. You've said you don't really remember anything about the day *before* the strike, but I clearly remember you in the outfield, the cloudy sky, worrying whether a storm would blow up and you'd have to end the game early.

"I was looking down at my phone when I saw a bright flash out of the corner of my eye, and heard a loud clap of thunder almost immediately. A parent next to me hollered out, 'My God, she's been struck by lightning!' When I looked up, I saw you on the ground, smoke sort of wafting off you. Your shoes had been blown off, and you just lay there, twitching. I screamed, jumped up, vaulted over the railing, and reached you before anyone else. They were all just standing there, gaping at you.

"I heard someone say, 'Don't touch her! She might shock you!' But that didn't make any sense to me, and I didn't care, anyway. I just needed to check on you. Your hair was singed, and the weirdest thing was that I could see a couple of toenails had been blown off like your shoes, and your foot looked like it had passed through a flame. The coaches came out on the field then, and a little later an ambulance came and took you to Foothills Children's ER."

Skye had listened quietly, but now said, "I'm sorry you went through all that, Mom, but I've heard you tell this before. And I know the trauma affected me, affected you. But I'm not sure what this has to do with whether you thought I was weirder than my friends."

"I'm getting to that. You were unconscious for a couple of weeks, and then you woke up, but you still didn't talk. You just stared into space. Once you started talking, it was like your words had been dammed up and they all needed to come out. A lot of it sounded like babbling. But after a couple of days, you started talking about other kids in the ICU. Do you remember that?"

"Not really. I mean, I remember having odd dreams, but I can't remember what they were. It's all hazy."

"There was one week in particular when you kept telling us about conversations with the other kids. **Your dad, your aunt, or I stayed with you 24/7,** and none of us ever saw any other kids come into your room, and you never left it. We found out at least a couple of the kids you named actually were in the ICU, but unconscious. So they couldn't have been talking with you. We just figured maybe you had heard their names, and you were dreaming about them.

"But then... one day you were telling us about a conversation you were in the middle of with one of them, and all of a sudden you stopped. Then you said, 'Timmy's gone away.' Just at that moment, we heard 'Code Blue! 511!' over the public address system, and all the nurses and doctors scrambled to the room right around the corner from yours, pushing a crash cart. We don't know what happened, but we saw weeping parents a little later."

Skye stared at the unicorn before responding. "Why can't I remember that? I can't remember any of that! What did you and Dad do?"

"We never talked about it with you. We probably should have, or at least should have talked with a hospital counselor or something. But it scared us. You had so much going on already, and anyway, the next week or so, you stopped talking about those conversations. It was like they never happened. So we just let it go."

"So, yeah, that was a little weird. Weirder than the average teenager. What happened after that?"

"You kept recovering, and seemed to forget about those conversations, and eventually you went home. But you had changed. You got quieter, less rambunctious. Not withdrawn, exactly, but in your own world more often. It felt like you wrapped a cloak around your heart, like you were afraid to let the world see the real you. We got used to that, gave you your space. And that's the way it was until you started college.

"We could see you start to blossom. You made friends, joined clubs, went to study groups. And then you started this job, and it was like the cloak got wrapped around again, only it felt different. Like you clutched the cloak tighter, and you made it thicker. It worried your dad and me. So that's why we came home a day early to surprise you. And that's why we brought you this unicorn."

Her mom studied Skye's face for a moment, looking for a clue to what went on inside. "Tell me I'm wrong?"

Skye sat quietly for a long time, and her mom waited patiently. Finally, she said, "It's back."

"What do you mean? What's back?"

"I'm having conversations with people who can't talk. I don't remember doing that before, but it fits with what's happening now. It's back. I wish I had known, or had remembered."

Mom looked worried. "Oh, honey! I'm so sorry. Is the job stressing you out too much? Should we... should we help you find someone to talk to?"

"Like who?"

"I don't know. A psychiatrist, maybe? Hallucinations can indicate a really serious condition."

"These aren't hallucinations, Mom! They're real!"

"I'm sure they feel real, sweetheart, but how can they be?"

"But I've been *helping* people with it! I helped a girl who has never spoken a word. I could hear her, and I was able to get her message to her nurses and doctors. She called me in the middle of the night to come save her, basically."

"She *called* you? On your cell phone? How?"

"No, not on my cell phone! She came to me in a dream and said she was in trouble."

Mom looked skeptical, but Skye continued.

"I helped a boy who was unconscious after an accident. He didn't know what had happened to him, and he was scared. I helped calm him down, Mom. I helped him! And Callie has helped me, too."

"Who's Callie?"

"She's ... well, it's complicated."

"So it seems."

"But she's been guiding me! And, anyway, I've been talking to a psychiatrist at the hospital. Well, not exactly a psychiatrist, but she's a counselor, and she knows what's happening with all this, and *she* doesn't think I'm crazy. She believes in me. Callie believes in me!" She paused, her lower lip quivering a little. "Can't you?"

Skye's phone buzzed at that moment. *Not now*, she thought, and started to put it away, but then saw the message from Tammy. "Back on tonight," it said. "Our friend is OK. Google 'pulmonary embolism.' You saved her."

Skye stood up suddenly.

"Skye, honey? Is everything OK?"

"Everything is more OK than you could know, Mom. I'm glad you're home, but I need to get out of here right now. But everything is really OK."

Skye went straight to her car with her mom following. Skye vaguely heard her making soothing sounds, worried sounds, but they didn't really register. *Saved*, she thought. *She said I saved Hope. I don't know if I did, but maybe I did. Maybe I made a difference. Maybe I can do something that matters.* She got in her car, waved to her mom, and took off.

She had been fortunate to find an efficiency in an old house that had been converted into apartments. Most of her neighbors in adjacent apartments were university students or people down on their luck. Her dad called it "the Rat Hole," and she had to admit it wasn't the most upscale of living situations, just a bedroom and a bathroom with a microwave oven beside the sink. But it was her space, and it let her save most of her salary to use toward getting a good degree.

As she drove there, another thought struck her. *If I really can do this, maybe I have to do it. I would be wrong not to do it, wouldn't I?* She turned that over in her mind. The business degree she had been pursuing no longer seemed like a good fit. But she didn't know of a degree program for... what was she? A psychic? A medium? How would she make a living? What would her friends, the few she had, think? What would her pastor think?

She pulled into the gravel parking lot behind the old house and sat in the car with the engine idling. *I have a lot to think about. I sure wish I could talk with Callie.*

***

Skye sat by herself at the corner table just after lunch. The crowd had thinned out, something she counted on. She needed some quiet time before going back to the fourth floor.

She kept watching for Callie as she nursed her coffee, but saw no sign of her. *I really need to talk with her about that conversation with Mom last night. I guess you can't make an appointment with your Muse.*

"Well, hello there, Skye!"

She turned to see Dan Roberts smiling at her. *He almost looks glad to see me,* she thought. She stood up, but he said, "No, no, no need to get up. Have a seat. May I join you?"

"Be my guest! How is Hope doing? Is she still in the ICU?"

"She is doing much better today. She had a close call the other night, but she's fine now."

They both sat down in awkward silence for a beat or two. The Dan said, "The truth is, I was hoping to find you here."

"What made you think I would hang out in the hospital café? Do I look like I need caffeine a lot?" She smiled, and Dan laughed. "Don't we all?" he said. "A hospital runs on caffeine, and the coffeemaker on the fifth floor is still broken. But there was another reason. It turns out I think we have a friend in common, and she has a tendency to work around coffee shops."

Skye said nothing, just kept watching Dan.

"Let me put it this way. Does the name 'Callie' mean anything to you?"

"It might. Tell me more."

Dan regarded her carefully neutral expression, deciding how to proceed.

"Did you know that I'm a writer and a speaker?"

"Not until recently. I just know you as Hope's dad. But, yeah, somebody mentioned it to me. What do you write and speak about?"

"For most of my life, it has been about effective communication, especially helping people speak effectively. But last year I wrote a book about figuring out your *why*, your reason for being on this earth—what makes your heart sing. You see, although I have enjoyed teaching college and speaking, my heart was really in writing, and it took some insights from Callie to help me see that. I finally changed my life's work focus after I retired from teaching.

I have another couple of books in progress now. I haven't stopped speaking, but now I speak to support my writing and help people use what I write."

"Figuring out your *why*. Huh. Boy, I sure could have used that recently."

"Are you trying to decide on a career or something like that?"

"Heck, I'm trying to figure out *why me*! I've had things happening to me that I don't understand, so instead of asking *why*, I'm asking *what the heck is happening to me? Why me!* Do you think your book would help me with *that*?"

As Skye talked, her voice had ramped up, becoming louder, her gestures more animated, so that other people in the café stopped talking and watched. She looked around, suddenly realizing she drew attention. "Sorry," she almost whispered. "But that's what I'm trying to decide. A career is the *last* thing on my mind right now. I'm just trying to decide whether I'm nuts."

Dan paused again, considering. When he finally spoke, he said, "Skye, I owe you an apology. I'm sorry if I've made things harder on you."

Skye said nothing, watching Dan warily.

"If you're nuts, so am I."

She raised her eyebrows, but she still said nothing.

"You haven't told me whether 'Callie' means anything to you, and I take that to mean you don't trust me yet. And I don't blame you. But maybe this will help, and if it doesn't, then you will definitely think I'm the one who's nuts, whether or not you are.

Callie, this mutual friend I suspect we have, has a tattoo inside her wrist in Greek letters. Yes?"

After a beat, Skye nodded silently.

"Other people don't see her, right?"

Skye hesitated, then nodded again.

"That tattoo? It's Greek for *poiesis*, a word that means 'creativi ty.'"

"Yeah, I've seen it."

Dan took a deep breath. "You know she's one of the Greek Muses, right?"

"Why would a *Greek* Muse appear to *me*? I'm not Greek! I'm not creative! I'm a Black American! If I'm getting a muse or a guardian or a guide or something, shouldn't it be African, or maybe Native American? What am I even saying?"

Dan smiled slightly, amused, and shrugged. "I can't even figure out why my wife does what she does, much less why a demigod does what a demigod does. I *do* know she has gone by other names, like an ancient Egyptian named Ptah or a Maori goddess named Hinewai. I'll bet she's appeared as an African deity at some point, and I know she claims the Native American name of Kokopelli. I was so surprised to see her again, I forgot to ask her how she decides how she'll show up."

"Again? You've seen her again?"

"Yep. Right here, in fact. I didn't think I would ever see her again, and she sat with me right where you're sitting now."

"When?"

"Just last Monday afternoon."

Skye gaped, her eye wide. "But she was with *me* all afternoon!"

"First of all, I will take that as a 'yes.'"

"OK, you got me. Yes, I know Callie, and yes, it's obvious we both know her."

"So either she's real or we're both nuts. I will reserve judgment on that, but I'll keep talking, since that's what I do. Second, from what she's told me before, she doesn't experience time the way you and I do, sort of like The Doctor[1]."

"Who?"

"Exactly. So if she experiences time happening all at once or in a different order than you and I do, I don't see any reason she couldn't be with you and with me at the same time—at least from our perspective. Make sense?"

"I... It makes as much sense as anything else that has happened to me the last couple of weeks. But that still leaves me asking: why *me*? What is happening to me?"

Dan opened his sketchbook to the page where he had written a brief note following his last conversation with Callie and turned it so Skye could read it.

"There's believing. And there's believing in," she read out loud. "What does that mean?"

"When I realized who had been talking with me as I worked through what became my book, I didn't believe it at first. I thought I had dreamed it all, especially when nobody else had seen her. Then she left me a note, one that had all the indications of having been written 300 years earlier, though it was addressed to me. The stuff in that note convinced me she was real, but I couldn't get my wife to believe it—until Grace read a note that Callie had left for her. I still don't know what that note said, but after she read it, she said she believed me.

"I've never told anyone else about Callie, since I knew no one would believe it. I did use her in a book, but I could pretend it was just fiction. But on Monday Callie helped me to see that it is not all that important whether someone believes I'm telling literal, factual-type truth. They know I'm a writer, so they assume I make things up. They have a point, by the way. Truth, actual truth, goes way beyond mere factuality. There are deeper truths. But I digress.

"Callie helped me see that even when Grace didn't believe me, she believed *in* me. Grace had faith in me as a writer. She believed I could achieve my dream even when I didn't.

"And I don't really know why Callie didn't just tell you this herself, but I think she wanted me to tell you that you have helped my daughter. I know I got protective. I was afraid to believe it. It doesn't fit my worldview, but then neither does getting a visit from a Greek demigod. But I know you helped Hope, and that's all that matters to me."

Skye looked down at her hands. "Callie did tell me. I just didn't believe her."

"Let me get this straight. You believed you could hear and talk with a child that no one else could hear or talk with..."

"Children," Skye interrupted. "There's more than one."

"...children no one else could hear or talk with, that a barista no one else saw or heard could impart wisdom to you..."

"To be fair, I didn't know no one else could see or hear her until Monday."

"But you found it out! You could believe those things, but you couldn't believe this person when she told you that you have a special gift? Because I'm pretty sure that's what she told you."

Skye smiled. "It sounds oddly stupid when you put it like that."

"Welcome to my world. I'm usually on the receiving end of conversations like this." Dan grinned lopsidedly. "So, Skye, here's the point. I believe in you. I do. And I think the sooner you believe in you too, the sooner the world will benefit from your uniqueness. Now, why don't you tell me about how you go about doing what you do?"

For the next three hours, or so it seemed, Skye told Dan all about what had happened with her in the preceding weeks—about her first conversation with Hope, about passing on the hint about the abdominal thing, about Charlie, about her own encounter with lightning and the ICU, about the midnight run to get help for Hope. (That story made Dan get teary. "I had a feeling you had something to do with it," he said, and went to get coffee for them both.) Dan just listened, and the more he listened without judgment or skepticism, the more Skye opened up, recounted, explored, questioned.

As Skye talked, the café around them darkened, faded away. They were alone. No sound intruded, not even the sound of the espresso machines or the HVAC. No one wandered by. The tables that remained visible sat empty. They did not notice, totally engaged with each other.

When Skye finished, she stopped and sat quietly. It felt to Dan not so much like she had exhausted the story, but that it had completed, like topping off a water jug and putting the cap on. They sat like that in silence for an indeterminate time. Slowly, the activity of the room came back, and the machines began humming, hissing, clicking, gurgling and popping again, accompanying the humming and buzzing of conversation. Skye suddenly realized how long they had been talking, and a momentary fear of getting in trouble for absence on the job crossed her mind. But she looked at the clock and saw she had only used 10 minutes of her break.

"That was powerful," Dan said. "You may not think you're creative, but you tell your story with great impact."

"You think it's a story?"

"I do, in the best possible sense of the word. I don't mean you made it up, or it's a lie, or anything. Whether it's factual, and I believe everything you're telling me *is* factual, a story is more than just a recounting of events. A story involves a character with a goal facing an obstacle or a challenge to that goal, with something at stake. In the process of tackling the challenge, the character grows or changes. You don't just *have* a story. You *are* a story. Your growth is amazing. And you haven't written the final chapter yet."

"So, what's next in my story?"

"I don't know. Let me reveal an open secret. It's an artificial distinction, but writers constantly have a mostly friendly argument about the writing process. You'll frequently hear them talk about being a plotter or a pantser—a writer who works without an outline. More politely, they'll talk about being a planner or a discovery writer. Most are actually a blend, but writers tend toward one end or the other of that spectrum.

"That works in writing. But in life? We're all pantsers. Some of us think we're plotters, but life has a way of changing things up.

"So I don't know where your story goes. I don't know how it ends. I suspect it's more of a novel than a short story. But I can tell you what it isn't. It isn't a recipe."

Skye nodded. "I have to admit, I would like some spoilers. But I'm getting comfortable with the plot unfolding."

"There is one thing I would ask of you, though."

Skye waited. Dan, once again, choked up. Finally, he squeezed out, "Would you please come to Hope's room, and if she is willing, would you please, please help me have a conversation with my daughter?"

Now Skye couldn't speak. They sat in tears together, and she just nodded. The two of them stood up, hugged, and together they left the café.

From the shadows of a corner, previously unseen, Callie came to the table. She picked up the empty coffee cups, produced a sparkling rag and wiped the table, adjusted the chairs, and took a step back. She nodded in satisfaction, smiled, and said, "Well, that went well. Let's see what sprouts from this seed." She gathered her materials and faded behind the counter.

One of the two people at a nearby table said, "Did you hear somebody talking?"

"Nah. Do you see anybody? It's probably just the ringing in your ears. Hurry up, we gotta get back to work."

***

Skye had to quickly empty trash and mop floors, but as soon as she could, she went to 509. Dan and Grace waited for her there. Erica had the day off, but she had left a note for Juanita, who gave them privacy.

"So, how do we do this?" Dan asked.

"To tell you the truth, I don't really know."

From the bed, Hope said, "For crying out loud, just start!"

Skye laughed, and said, "I think Hope may be in charge of this."

Grace joined in the laughter. "Let me tell you something. Hope has *always* been in charge, ever since she came along." She turned to look at Dan, looked back at Skye, and tears welled up in her eyes. "I'm still not sure I believe this, but I've seen a lot that I had trouble believing that I've had to accept. And...." Her voice got thick, and she barely managed to continue. "....I've waited her entire life hoping for something like this."

Skye spent the next four hours acting as a channel between Hope and her parents. They laughed and cried together. Hope happily twirled around the room's ceiling, practically dancing on air, while her mom raised her wheelchair high enough to hold her physical hand and her dad held the other. Skye didn't notice when the floor supervisor called Environmental Technology to ask that someone else come upstairs to deal with some of the other rooms—she was too involved with the conversation to notice, and none of them thought about lunch or any sort of break.

Finally, though, Skye stumbled a little, having stood up the entire time, and Dan noticed she looked ashen.

"Are you OK, Skye?"

"I'm not sure. I think this takes more out of me than I realized."

"Your cloud looks a little frazzled, Skye," Hope said.

"My what?"

"That's what I call the colors I see around people. I think when their real selves and their bodies work together, people have something like the rainbows I've seen on TV around them. Yours is sort of fluttery. I think you need a nap. So do I."

Skye sat down and said, "I should probably quit for today. Would it be OK if we talked some more another day?"

Both Dan and Grace immediately agreed, concerned about Skye's well-being. "Thank you for understanding, but thank you for letting me help here. I believe, though, I need to clock out and go home."

Chapter Six

Crisis

Irene greeted Skye with a cup of hot tea. She had soothing music playing at low volume, and a reed diffuser releasing lavender into the air.

"So, what's been going on with you this week? I imagine Monday was a big day."

"To say the least. More has happened this week than in the previous month."

"I texted you on Tuesday to see how things were going, and I will admit I worried a bit when I didn't hear from you."

"I know. I'm sorry about that. I still had things to process, and I really didn't want to dig into it too much. I should have let you know."

"That's OK! I don't want to add to your stress, just support you. But I have to say, as you walked in here today, there is an entirely different feeling around you. Have you come to some sort of resolution?"

"You could say that. I still don't quite know where things are going, but after I saw you Monday, Callie and I went for a walk. We had quite an involved talk that left me questioning things in a whole different way. I got a 'visit' from Hope while I slept that led to, I guess, me saving Hope's life. Then I ran into Hope's dad in the café, where all this seems to have played out. We had a long, deep discussion. I found out that he knows Callie! And then yesterday I went to Hope's room, and I helped Hope talk to her mom and dad for the first time ever."

"Whoa, back up a minute. What do you mean, he knows Callie?"

"She's his Muse."

"Muse? I'm lost."

"You know, one of the Greek Muses. Literally. You said she felt different, and I guess that's why. She's not dead, she's totally alive, she just lives on a different plane or something. I don't know. I'm still trying to understand it, but that's what she is."

Irene looked slightly stunned. "OK, I've never run into anything like this. I mean, given my own experience, I have worked with other people who can communicate with folks who have passed on, but…. This sounds like a mythical being of some sort. And you know mythical beings aren't people who are alive or dead. They've never really existed at all!"

Skye stared at Irene. "Don't tell me that now *you* don't believe me."

"No, no, it's not that at all! I'm just trying to wrap my head around what's happening." Irene gathered her thoughts. "Let me probe your experience a bit, just to get a better sense of it. Clearly, I sensed someone there with us. You could see her, though, right?"

"Yes."

"Was it like when you could see Hope and Charlie?"

"Not really. I mean, I could always tell the difference between them and their physical bodies, except for that first time with Hope. It's almost like in the movies when they show someone's ghost. They looked sort of milky, and you could see through them a little. I took a course once in Photoshop, and it was like having a layer set at 70 percent transparency. Callie seemed as solid as you and me."

"What did she look like?"

Skye thought back. "She was a little taller than me, with long, curly hair tending toward a sort of bronze color. I remember her looking tanned, but with a glowing quality. Not much makeup, just naturally pretty. And she was wearing one of the food service uniforms. I can't remember if she had a badge or not, but the shoulder patch clearly said Foothills Children's Hospital Food Service."

"You would not expect a Greek demigod to wear that, would you?"

"Exactly! That's one reason it was such a surprise when you couldn't see her."

"So what makes you think she's one of the Greek Muses? Nine of them, right?"

"Yeah, I think she said she had eight sisters. I think she's one of those because that's what she told me. I either believe that, or I have to discount all of it. If I'm doubting that, I have to doubt we're even having this conversation right now, and that's just getting too woo-woo, too existential."

Irene smiled. "I'm almost channeling Dr. Harrison again. Reality behaves as if it's out there. So let's just say that's a given. I certainly feel like I'm actually here. So let's go back. You said that Hope's dad already knew Callie, or something like that?"

"Yes. I didn't learn a lot about the details. When we talked, now that I think about it, it was mostly me doing the talking. But he said she had helped him write his book—especially the first one. He said he knew she helped him all the time, but he only saw her and talked with her during a short period."

Irene pursed her lips, looked at the ceiling for a moment. "So, why was he having that conversation with you? Why were you talking about Callie?"

"At first, I wasn't sure whether I could trust him. After all, he was the reason I thought I had to leave the ICU. But he said Callie had come to him again, and he realized he needed to apologize to me. And he did! He showed me something he had written after his talk with Callie. It said, 'There's believing. And there's believing in.' And he said I needed to believe in myself, that it was more important than believing something merely factual."

Irene smiled slightly and said, "Where have I heard that before?"

Skye smiled back. "I get it. That's what you've been telling me all along. They say great minds think alike."

"I think it's a message you needed to hear from a lot of different sources. Is that why I sensed a different feeling around you today?"

"Probably so. For one thing, I have asked if I could go back to the ICU. They're going to transfer me back on Monday. I don't know what will happen after that, but I know I can't run away from this. I just have to figure out what to do with it."

Irene nodded. "I understand that. For whatever it's worth, I had to figure out something similar when I realized I could sense things beyond the surface. I didn't want to get a crystal ball and start reading palms, that sort of thing. But I found I could use my abilities in lots of ways that were more, shall we say, conventional.

"So, tell me about bridging Hope and her parents. In my line of work, I would say you 'facilitated the conversation.'"

"That sounds so clinical! I can tell you it felt more satisfying than anything I've done in the last week, but it took a lot out of me. I'm surprised how it exhausted me! But it was a good exhaustion. I mean, they've been deeply in each other's lives for 20 years, but in a lot of ways it felt like they met for the first time. They had tons of questions for each other. Since Hope has heard them for her whole life, she knew a lot of surface stuff about her parents, but she had lots and lots of questions about 'why,' and what some things meant—like, she's seen a lot of things on TV, and she's real familiar with the route from her house to her doctors' offices and hospital, but she didn't know what a country is, or what politics is and why people get so angry about it. And her parents had lots of questions about what Hope likes and doesn't like, what she experiences, what she can and can't do. We talked for hours, but they have *days* and *weeks* of conversations to have, and I ran out of steam and had to quit. I hope I can help them lots more, but I don't think the hospital is going to want to have me spending my time that way. But there must be bunches of people out there needing someone who can, what did you call it? 'Facilitate a conversation'?"

"So, what's next?"

"I'm not sure. It's a different 'not sure' than where I was last week, but I'm not sure."

Irene chuckled. "I don't mean to treat you like a kid. You're well beyond that. But part of me wants to say, 'Welcome to adulthood, sweetheart!'"

Skye laughed. "I'm figuring that part out, too. I used to think adults had everything figured out. I wanted to get to that stage so I could have the confidence that comes from knowing how things worked, knowing what to expect, et cetera. I'm figuring out that people make plans to give themselves direction, but that you should hold those plans lightly. That, really, you're figuring things out as you go. Right?"

"That's pretty close. Like, I knew when I got up this morning that you and I would meet today. I didn't know I would talk about a mythical being with you."

"Who'd a thought?" They both laughed. "Anyway, I'm pretty sure I don't want to go around talking to everybody about this. But I can't just shove it under a rug either. But they don't have a major in 'coma communication' or 'new age channeling' or whatever."

"Here's a thought: maybe social work?"

"Are you recruiting now? This would make an interesting video pitch!"

"I'm always looking for people who can help make the world a better place through social work," Irene said with a smile. "But you have many channels available, no pun intended. I think you probably need someone who can guide you as you develop your abilities, help keep you safe as you do. What kind of interaction have you had with Callie since Monday?"

Skye looked wistful. "Honestly, I haven't seen her at all. I've been to the café every day, hoping to catch her. That's why I was there on Wednesday, when I talked with Mr. Roberts. But she hasn't shown up, and when I asked someone about her, they just looked at me strangely and said they had nobody by that name or description working there."

She looked out the window for a moment, and her lower lip quivered. "I'm afraid she's gone. I'm afraid I'll never see her again. Just when I need her the most."

Irene leaned forward and took Skye's hand gently. "First, I don't think she's abandoned you, which is what it seems like you're feeling. In fact, I think maybe she was with you *exactly* when you needed her most. Maybe that's why she appeared when she did. And while I respect your feeling, maybe you're not seeing her now because you *don't* need her that way anymore. Does that make sense?"

"I don't want it to make sense. But I guess it does."

"And here's another thing, and let me slip out of social worker mode for a moment. You remember that although I couldn't see her in the café, I could sense her presence? That I didn't get the same feeling I get with someone who is no longer alive on this plane. But I could sense her?"

"Yes, I remember that."

"Well. I'm sensing that now, that same 'fill the room' feeling. Ever since you walked in here. So I don't think she has abandoned you."

Skye looked quickly around the room. "I don't see her!"

"I wouldn't expect you to. When I sense a presence like that, I usually get a sense of location, like, 'She's behind you,' or 'He's over there by the potted plant.' I'm not getting that right now. I'm just getting that she's here, and it's focused around you, wherever you go in this room. I think, in some way, Callie comes through you, that Callie *is* you, or you are Callie."

"Are we talking about reincarnation now? This is getting wilder and wilder. Like, I was a demigod in a previous life or something?"

"It's not exactly that. It's hard to explain. It's more like Callie comes from you, but you come from Callie, too. I think I can definitely say that she has not abandoned you. You're getting exactly what you need, when you need it."

"OK, maybe. I have some other questions, more to help me understand what I see and hear."

"I'll help you the best I can. Whatever you're experiencing, it's different from what I experience. But I have some friends who are sensitive in different ways, so I may be able to clarify some things."

"So, the first time I talked with Hope, I only saw one of her, but now I have no trouble differentiating a physical Hope and one I can see, but who looks sort of see-through to me. Why did it change?"

"I can't say for sure, although I can tell you my own sensitivities shifted as I got used to them. I suspect that when you first held a conversation with Hope, your brain tried to make sense of the experience, and so you only saw the one interacting with you. As your sensitivity increased, you could tell the difference between the physical body and what my friends would call the astral body or the energetic body. Does that seem to make sense?"

"Yeah, I guess so. It's at least easier to say 'astral Hope' than 'translucent Hope,' which is how I've thought of her. But I'm not just seeing two versions of Hope or Charlie. The astral version seems connected to the physical version with something that looks sort of like a tube or a cable or a wire. It's not real obvious, but if I concentrate, I can see it."

"One of my friends does something she calls 'astral projection,' and I've heard her describe something like that. She calls it a 'silver cord,' but she also says ancient Sanskrit has a word for it: *sutratma*. Different traditions all over the world talk about a similar concept. It's even referenced in Ecclesiastes in the Jewish Bible, what you would probably call the Old Testament. That sounds like what you're talking about."

"It reminds me of an umbilical cord."

"That's a pretty good comparison. My astral projector friend says it's really important, that the sutratma keeps you connected until you die. In fact, some say that if it breaks while you're projecting, you can't get back."

Skye sat back in her chair, looking worried. "I'm not sure how I feel about that."

"What a coincidence! I was going to ask you how you feel about that." She smiled, and Skye relaxed. "It's a lot to process, and I think you have a lot to think about. That's probably enough for this week, don't you think? Same time next week?"

***

When the doors opened from the ambulance bay and they rolled the gurney in, Jessica knew her shift would be intense. Not that there was ever a shift in the ER that was not. After all, she wanted to work there *because* of its intensity. She thrived on the adrenaline, the diversity, the never-knowing what would come through the doors. Lately, she had spent way too much time dealing with RSV and other respiratory ailments—just starting the season, and already it threatened to overwhelm the hospital in general and the ER in particular.

So while she didn't wish catastrophe on anyone, she welcomed a new challenge when it came. Still, this one looked over the top.

They had a half dozen cases all come in at once. Jessica's patient was an eight-year-old girl named Lakisha. Jessica looked over the records from the intake triage.

On a regular Sunday evening, little Lakisha began to feel unwell. A dull ache in her tummy surfaced, but she dismissed it as just the consequence of eating her dinner too quickly. As the hours ticked by, however, the pain in her stomach sharpened and became more relentless.

She had a restless night, with a fever inducing chills despite her warm covers. Her forehead felt hot to the touch, and she moaned about a general achiness that made her softest pajamas feel made of rough twine.

By morning, nausea had washed over her. Her favorite breakfast of pancakes now turned her stomach, leading to an episode of vomiting. She couldn't keep any of her food down, and even small sips of water seemed to stir up discomfort. Her mother, concerned by this sudden illness, took her temperature, registering a worrying 101.5° F.

As the day wore on, Lakisha's symptoms took a turn for the worse. She suffered from severe diarrhea, unusually liquid and tinged with blood. The stomach cramps became so intense, they made her double over in pain. She felt drained and lacked the energy to engage in her usual activities—a stark difference from her usual vibrant, lively self.

Her appetite completely disappeared, and her mother noted that she urinated less frequently. Her normally warm, rich skin tone now appeared dull and ashen. Her vibrant cheeks, usually full of life, seemed sallow and drawn in, a clear sign of her deteriorating health. Despite the coolness of the day, she felt parched, attempting to replenish the fluids her body was rapidly losing.

When her symptoms showed no signs of abating after a few hours, her mother, filled with anxiety, rushed her to the emergency room. The swift onset of symptoms, their severity, and the fact that they didn't subside indicated something seriously amiss. By the time they arrived, Lakisha had slipped into unconsciousness.

Her pulse ran like a race car, and her blood pressure had dropped precipitously.

Jessica easily inserted an IV for Lakisha as her mother sat close by, chewing on her nails, never taking her eyes off her daughter. "I just feel so helpless!" she said.

"You made the right decision. If you had waited even another couple of hours, things could have become much worse."

"They don't look good right now."

"Dr. Richardson will be in soon to look things over. Can I get you anything?"

"No, thanks. Just... just save my baby! I've never seen her like this!"

"We will do everything we can. I know this is really stressful, but we will do our best for your child."

"I know you will." She nervously kneaded the ball of shredded tissue in her hands.

A woman in a white lab coat with a stethoscope around her neck came in while Jessica finished taping the IV in place. "Mrs. Tidewell, I'm Dr. Richardson. I'll be taking care of your daughter for the next little bit. We are running a battery of blood tests right now to determine exactly what is going on. Can you tell me if Lakisha has been any place out of the ordinary in the last few days?"

"She went on a school field trip last Thursday. That's the only thing unusual."

"Where did they go?"

"They went to a farm north of town. Most of the kids have never seen farm animals at all except on TV, and they had a chance to visit, thanks to one of the parents."

"Did the farm happen to be Valley View Sheep Station?"

"Yes, that was it. I had forgotten the name."

Dr. Richardson and Jessica exchanged glances. "Mrs. Tidewell, Lakisha is one of five students we have treated within the past twenty-four hours with the same symptoms. They all appear to have been on the same field trip. Based on what we've seen from others, I'm going to order some additional tests. I have a feeling I know what this is, but I need to verify before moving forward with any new treatment"

Dr. Richardson turned to Jessica. "Jess, I'll watch for the records to come back, but if you see the results first, let me know immediately. I'm particularly watching for the outcome of the BUN and creatinine tests. Also, the series of coagulation studies. The CBC showed anemia, so we could be dealing with HUS."

"I'll keep an eye out."

Two hours passed with Jessica constantly in and out, checking on both Lakisha and her mom. Then Jessica brought Irene into the room.

"Hello, Mrs. Tidewell, I'm Irene, and I'm one of the social workers here at Foothills Children's Hospital. I wanted to check in with you since this is a really stressful time for you. Jessica thought I might be of help. Is it OK if we talk a bit?"

"Yes, thank you. But call me Sasha. 'Mrs. Tidewell' makes me feel old."

While they talked, Dr. Richardson came back in. "We are finding definite signs of hemolytic uremic syndrome. That can be an effect of a severe infection, and an early culture of other blood tests suggest Lakisha has a serious E. coli infection. Do you know if Lakisha interacted with the sheep at all?"

"She said something about petting and playing with a sheep. She was excited about it! Did she pick up an infection just from that?"

"Unfortunately, probably so. We're not only seeing it right now, but we're bracing for an influx. The school will alert all the parents in the morning. In any case, we need to take her upstairs to the ICU. We'll be able to constantly monitor her and get her the treatment she will need."

"Isn't there some antibiotic that will help with this?"

"Unfortunately, no. We really don't have an effective treatment for E. coli, at least not directly. The best we can do is to manage the symptoms until it has worked its way through. It's almost certain Lakisha will need dialysis..."

Sasha gasped as if someone had punched her.

"...but that's not likely to have to continue for very long, a few weeks, just until we get her kidneys working again. We'll be running IV fluids to help with dehydration. If we need to transfuse her, do you have any religious objections?"

"Transfuse? You mean, give her blood? Is it that bad?"

"Not yet, but we need to be prepared, just in case. We wouldn't do it without checking with you first, but it would help if we knew about treatment limitations."

"You do what you need to do for my little girl, no problem. Is she going to be all right?"

"We're going to do our best to make sure she is. We have already notified the ICU, and their folks are coming down right now to help with the transfer."

"I need to call her daddy right now. What room will she be in?"

"You can tell him to come to room 510. We'll move her while you're making your calls. Jessica?"

"Erica just got here. We'll get her taken care of."

They quickly gathered the monitors and IV poles along with the gurney and wheeled Lakisha to the staff elevator in the back of the ER. As they rode up, Jessica whispered to Erica, "Is that gal you were telling me about working today? The one who can talk to the unconscious?"

"Not only is she working, but it's her first day back in the ICU. She was working on another floor, but she's back with us now, and I'm glad, especially since it sounds like we might have more of these to deal with. Poor kid."

"You know it! No eight-year-old should have to deal with stuff like this."

"I agree, but I was actually talking about Skye. I have a feeling she has no idea what she's in for."

***

Erica saw Skye coming out of 518 with her cart and hurried over. "Am I glad to see you! I heard you were coming back, but they sent somebody else up to cover the floor yesterday."

"I called out yesterday. I am sooooo far behind on school work, I just had to catch up. I hated to, since they had already assigned me up here, but I really can't afford to flunk out."

"I understand, but I think we have a bunch of new patients who need your intervention. They're probably feeling lost and scared. In fact, Irene came up here a little while ago, looking for you."

Erica quickly filled Skye in on the mass infection facing the children, including the potential for extremely dire consequences, and Skye's anxiety began to grow. Already, she could feel the fear emanating from several rooms, hear questioning voices at the edge of her consciousness. As her doubt threatened to spill over, Irene came through the unit back doors and, upon spotting Skye, immediately brightened.

"There you are!" she said. "I was hoping you would be here. Dr. Powell is on today, and he agrees with me that we should see if you can provide any useful insights—unofficially, of course. Are you up for that?"

"Honestly, I'm not sure. This sounds big! What if it's too much and I can't handle it? Wouldn't it be better to just let the doctors do their thing?"

"Trust me, the doctors and nurses are already 'doing their thing,' and they'll continue. Don't worry, Skye, you don't have it all hanging from your shoulders. You're just providing a little additional insight, if you can. And if you can't, then nothing is lost. Dr.

Powell will just be in the same place he would have been without you. No pressure, OK? Let's just see what comes out of it. Make sense?"

Skye took a deep breath. "OK. I'll do what I can."

Lakisha's mom looked up as Irene and Skye entered 510. "Sasha, this is the young lady I was telling you about in the ER. She is working today in the ICU, and I thought it would be a good opportunity to bring her in."

Sasha looked Skye up and down, lingering on the Environmental Services nametag and the mop she still carried. "I think I saw you cleaning the bathroom earlier, didn't I? You're not a nurse or a social worker?"

"No, ma'am. I'm an Environmental Technician. I guess you could say I'm a housecleaner."

"But don't let that fool you, Sasha," Irene said. "As I told you, Skye not only is a former ICU patient herself, she experienced something similar to what Lakisha is experiencing, and the staff here has learned that she has a, for lack of a better term, special connection with the children who come through here."

"And Dr. Powell is OK with this?"

"Dr. Powell knows her track record. I wouldn't say this is the usual course of treatment for Foothills Children's. Let's just say it's a bit of extra wellbeing support. Wouldn't you say so, Skye? ... Skye?"

"Oh, sorry! It's just that Lakisha is shouting so loud, I couldn't really follow what you were saying. I really should talk with her, if I may."

Lakisha's mom looked confused, but said, "Go ahead, if you can."

Skye stepped to the bed beside the still form lying there, hooked up to monitors and tubes and IVs. She noticed that Lakisha's pulse hovered around 110.

"Lakisha," she said. "I can hear you. I can even see you. But no one else in the room can, and that's why your mom isn't answering. There is no need to be afraid. My name is Skye, and I'm going to help you communicate with your mom, your nurse, and your doctor. OK?"

"I thought maybe I was dreaming all this!" a translucent version of Lakisha said. "I have been trying all night to get somebody to hear me. Can you hear me now?"

"Yes, I can. No need to shout now."

The others in the room only heard Skye's side of the conversation. Lakisha's mom watched intently. She leaned over and whispered to Irene, "Why is she looking above Lakisha instead of at her?"

Skye turned to Sasha and said, "I'm looking where I see Lakisha. To me, it looks like she's sitting up in bed, and I'm looking into her eyes." Turning back to Lakisha, she said, "Honey, you are a very sick girl. So your body needs to use all its energy to heal itself, and that leaves your mind free to roam around a little. Do you ever fly when you dream?"

"Sure! Doesn't everybody?"

"I don't know about that, but I know I do. I just don't remember it very often. And you might not remember this conversation later, and if you do, you might think you were dreaming. But this part of you is awake. That part of other people is still all tied up in their bodies, so they can't hear you or see you. I don't really know why, but I'm able to see and hear you, and so I can help you communicate with them. Is that OK?"

"Can you please tell Mom I want her to switch back to that Disney movie, the one about that waitress who turns into a frog?"

Skye chuckled, and said, "I think she wants to watch *The Princess and the Frog*. Sounds like you were watching it earlier and switched to something else?"

Sasha looked surprised. "We *were* watching that before you came in. It's one of her favorites, but I figured she couldn't watch it anyway, so I changed it."

Irene looked at Sasha and raised an eyebrow. "Before we came in?"

Sasha sat silent for a moment, and said, "OK, maybe there's something to this." She turned to the still figure on the bed and said, "Honey, what else you want to tell us?"

Skye listened for a bit, and then said, "She says she doesn't want anybody to be mad at the sheep. It's not *their* fault."

Sasha silently watched Lakisha's still form, then her lips quivered, breaking into a smile, followed by a full-throated laugh. Skye and Irene laughed along with her, and it took her a minute to catch her breath. Finally, she said, "Sorry about that, it's just that things have been so tense, that really broke me open. That is *exactly* what I would expect that girl to say. Of course, she's gonna be worried about the sheep."

Sasha looked thoughtful. "She's been out of it ever since she got here. So she hasn't heard anything about sheep. Are you sure you didn't get that off her records or something?"

Skye turned to Lakisha, appeared to listen, then turned back to Sasha. "She says she heard that doctor talking with you about the sheep farm."

Irene said, "Skye hasn't seen Lakisha's record at all, Mrs. Tidewell. Since she's not medical staff, she can't look at them. HIPPA disallows that."

"Hmmmph. OK, maybe. What else is she saying?"

Skye looked back to Lakisha, who said, "There was a girl in here earlier, wearing a hospital gown. My mom couldn't see her or hear her, I think, but I could, and she could hear and see me. She said she was in the room next door, and that I shouldn't be afraid. But I was anyway."

"That sounds like Hope."

"Who is Hope?" Sasha asked.

"A patient in 509, next door," Irene explained. "Skye has talked with her, too."

"She told me not to be afraid," Lakisha said. "But then when she left, she didn't go out the door. She went through that wall over there, and that freaked me out! That's when I started shouting."

"I don't blame you. That would have freaked me out, too. Is there anything you want me to pass on to your mom or your nurse?"

"Do you know how long I will be here?"

"I don't think anyone knows, sweetie. The doctors and nurses are still figuring out just how sick you are."

"Could I get some ice cream?"

Skye chuckled. "That sounds good, but remember, you're unconscious. Or at least your body is. You can't eat anything right now."

Lakisha uttered a profanity she didn't expect to hear from an eight-year-old. Skye raised her eyebrows. "What did you say?" Lakisha repeated it, then said, "I would really like some *!#*ing ice cream."

"Where have you heard words like that, Lakisha?"

"From my daddy. He talked like that when he was mad before he left. I think he and mom fought about money. Anyway, I heard him say that, and now I'm mad, too."

"What's going on?" Sasha asked.

"Ummm, well, Lakisha says she wants some ice cream."

"Looked like she said something that shocked you. Ice cream don't sound shocking."

"It wasn't the ice cream. It was what she said when she got upset that she couldn't have it."

"What did she say?"

"She used a bad word she said she learned from her daddy."

"From Leonard? What, exactly, did she say?"

Skye hesitated, then repeated exactly what Lakisha had said.

Irene raised both eyebrows. Sasha covered her open mouth. Then she frowned, eyebrows knit together.

"Look, I don't know what you're trying to pull, but you can't make me believe this is legit. Next, you'll be trying to get my credit card number or something. You pretending to know something about Leonard, aren't you? Are you one of them?"

Skye looked horrified. "No, no, not at all! I'm just trying to help!"

"The best way you can help is to leave us alone! Things are hard enough right now without people like you trying to take advantage of people like me." She looked at Irene. "Are you really a hospital employee? How could you even be a party to this?"

Skye was practically in tears, but Irene remained calm. "I understand this is hard to accept, and I'm sorry to have added to your stress. I assure you, we only sought to help, but it is entirely up to you whether this is helpful—and obviously, it is not right now. Please accept my apologies! We will leave you alone now."

Irene gently took Skye's arm and steered her out of the room. Erica waited just outside the door.

"I get the feeling that did not go well," she said.

"To say the least," Irene replied. "I'm worried about the impact on mom and on Lakisha, but I'm also more than a little worried about our friend here."

Skye said nothing, just looked at the floor with her arms wrapped around, hugging herself. Irene said, "Skye, honey. You did your best. Not everyone is going to accept what you have to offer."

"Why should I even try? I didn't make things better for Lakisha. I made things worse. I can still hear her trying to get through to her mother, and she is really upset!" She turned toward 509 and said, "Not now, Hope! I have more to deal with than I can manage."

Erica and Irene exchanged glances. Irene said, "I think we need to go get some coffee. Who knows, maybe Callie will be there with some wisdom to share."

"I don't know if I even want to see her. She got me into this."

"Well, at least we can get some good coffee. Let's try it."

"I'll do what I can to calm things down," Erica said. "Dr. Powell won't be happy about this, though. He supports anything that will help, and he knows now that a lot of the useful observations the last few weeks have really come from Skye, but he also knows how much trouble could come from, shall we say, using unconventional treatment."

Skye clamped her hands on her temples. "How many unconscious children are in here right now?"

"Hope isn't exactly unconscious, but you know that," Erica said. "Along with Lakisha, we have four others who have the severe e. Coli infection. Three of them are unconscious. Why?"

"They're all crying, trying to get someone's attention! Lakisha is calling for me to come back, and Hope... I think Hope is talking to them all, trying to calm them, but they're all talking at once, and Lakisha told them I can hear them. I can't shut them out! I have to get out of here!"

She turned and ran for the door, still carrying her mop. Irene walked rapidly after her, head down, reluctant for parents to see multiple hospital staff running through the ICU. Dr. Powell stuck his head out from the back of the nurses' station. "What in blazes is going on?" he said. Erica shrugged helplessly and turned back to 510 to try to mitigate the damage.

***

Skye didn't quite know where she was running, just that she had to run. The voices in her head followed her, pleading for help, asking what was happening, crying for parents to respond. Before Irene rounded the corner from the ICU back entrance, Skye had darted into the alcove for the "front" staff elevator and entered it just as the doors closed. Seeking air and open space, she hit the button for the roof.

Surely some distance will quiet them, she thought. But the voices continued.

The doors opened, and Skye stepped out into the glass enclosed lobby and immediately pushed through to the open roof with the helipad. The wind hit her like slamming into a wall, nearly snatching the mop out of her hands. The hospital was taller than most of the adjacent buildings, all of them straddling a ridge above the city. Nothing stood in the way of the winds cascading down into the valley from the surrounding mountains. The roar of wind in her ears couldn't drown out the insistent voices that continued to call to her.

Reeling, she stumbled to the edge where the wind almost lifted her over the knee-high parapet. She looked out over the roofs of the neighboring buildings, the maze of streets running through the neighborhood. *This feels like a dream. Maybe it all* is *a dream.*

Skye remembered flying with Hope, the freedom and exhilaration she felt. *If this is a dream, I should be able to fly.*

The cacophony in her head continued.

She stepped up on the top of the parapet and moved her arms in a dog paddle, dropping her mop back onto the roof.

The mop handle hit the roof with a loud *thwack*, and Skye found herself standing on a white plain, stretching to the horizon in every direction she could see. The cacophony immediately ceased as well, yielding to a quiet deeper than she had ever experienced, not even containing the unconscious awareness of the sound of her own heartbeat, of blood rushing through her inner ear. Fearing she had gone suddenly deaf, she snapped her fingers and heard it impossibly clearly.

"What do you think you're doing?" said a voice right behind her, as if right on her neck though she felt nothing. Spinning around, she saw Callie, dressed not in her food service uniform, but in a flowing purple gown bound at the waist by a golden cord. Her hair, which she always had gathered at the back of her neck in a ponytail, now cascaded like a bronze waterfall down to her waist, bound by a diadem headband. In her left hand, she carried a lyre. She propped her right hand on her hip and tapped her foot.

"I said, what do you think you're doing?"

Skye looked all around, then back at Callie. "Me?"

Callie rolled her eyes. "Who else would I be talking to when it's just you and me on an infinite plain?"

Skye blinked. "I... well, really, I don't know what I'm doing. I'm right at the edge, I think."

"In more ways than one. Didn't Irene say you were reality challenged? Honey, if you take another step in the real world, you are going to find out the hard way the nature of incorporating into physical reality."

Skye looked all around, suddenly frightened, and back up to Callie. "I'm scared to move."

"Move all you want to here. You are safe in this place. But when you go back, you have to be very careful if you're going to keep your soul and body together. You want to do that, don't you?"

"Suddenly, I very much want to. Now that I'm here, wherever here is, I can get quiet enough in my head to think."

"I'm glad to hear that. I'll let you in on a secret. You can come here anytime you want."

"How? Do I have to go up on a roof and whack something every time I need quiet?"

"Impudence. Good. That's a good sign. No, you don't have to find a roof. You don't even have to click your heels or anything. But this quiet place is inside you, and you can access it when you need to. When you need it, you'll figure it out. And, evidently, you needed it right now."

"If I do, are you going to be waiting here for me?"

"Silly. I'm *always* with you. You just may not see me or hear me. From what I can see, that may be a good thing. Looks like seeing and hearing too much is the reason you're up on this roof."

"I just... I just had to get away from it all. I'm not sure I can do this, Callie. Or should I call you Calliope? I'm still having some issues with the whole Greek thing."

"Is that hanging you up? OK, let's try a different approach."

Before her eyes, Callie changed, morphing into a taller, darker woman. When she stabilized, Skye saw a young Black woman like herself, wearing a leopard print gown topped by an usekh broad collar around her neck. She held a quill pen in her right hand, with gold arm bands on both upper arms. A point of light, like a star, shined from a point on her forehead. Around her torso, she had a colorful drape like a shawl.

"If you'd rather, you can call me Seshat, Egyptian rather than Greek. I'm whatever you need so you can be the fullest *you* that you can be. You said you had to get away. You can get away from a lot of things, but you can never get away from being *you*. All you can do is delay it.

"You certainly have that right and ability," Seshat continued, "but there are lots of people who are counting on you to be *you*."

"I know. I think that's what freaked me out. They're counting on me, more so than ever now, but maybe I can't help them. Maybe they're wrong."

At that moment, another figure peaked around from behind Callie/Seshat. In her energy body now, Hope looked more solid than Skye had ever seen her since their first conversation. She waved almost shyly. "Hi, Skye. I'm sorry if we freaked you out."

Skye mellowed immediately and smiled. "That's OK, honey. It's just taking me a little time to figure things out."

"I know what you mean. I've been figuring things out for ages!"

"Are you OK being this far away from your room?"

"I think so. I think this is sort of like dreamworld, and I can go all over the place there. But I think this lady helped me get here. Did you, lady?"

Seshat smiled, reached down and stroked Hope's hair. "I helped a little. But you mostly did this yourself."

"I did, didn't I? But you shined a light for me."

"And you wanted to follow it, didn't you?"

"Yes. I felt like the light called me, and I came a long way, and this isn't the dreamworld. Will I remember this?"

"I don't know, honey. But I know you will make a difference while you're here."

Hope suddenly looked serious. "Skye needs me, doesn't she?"

Tears ran down Skye's cheeks, but Seshat kept smiling at Hope. "Yes, she does, sweetheart."

"That's OK. I will go talk with her."

Hope skipped to where Skye stood and took her hand.

"Skye, you helped me when I really needed you. And you helped my friend Charlie when he needed you, too. He and I have been playing in the dreamworld, and he told me you made him feel better when he was so scared. You tried to help Lakisha, and I know her mom scared you. But that's just because her mom was scared, too. I could see the light around her turning dark and murky, and I think she was already scared about what would happen to Lakisha. But Lakisha wants you to come back."

"I don't know if I can go back to Lakisha, Hope. Her mom may not let me."

"You don't worry about that. I'm going to help you with that."
Hope smiled confidently, and despite her misgivings, Skye felt
reassured, and smiled back. Hope continued, "You are the first
regular person I've ever been able to talk with, ever! A lot of my
nurses have sort of connected with me, some more than others. I
think you have to really care about people to be a nurse, and that
lets me feel a little connection. But ... I'm trying to think how to
tell you."

Hope looked around, frowning, as if trying to locate something,
then looked at Seshat and brightened up. "Say, lady, could I borrow
that wrap you have around your arms?"

Wordlessly, Seshat spun the shawl-like fabric behind her and
handed it to Hope, who took it and wrapped it around Skye's right
hand like a cross between a bandage and a boxing glove.

"There. Now it's hard for you to feel anything with that hand,
right?" Skye nodded. "Now close your eyes." Skye complied.

"If I take your hand in both of mine and squeeze, you can tell
something is happening, and you may even tell which way I'm
pushing, but you don't feel much, right?"

Again, Skye nodded, keeping her eyes tightly closed. "I really
couldn't tell you were holding my hand unless you moved back
and forth."

Hope unwrapped most of it until only a couple of layers covered
Skye's hand. "When I hold your hand now, you can feel a lot more,
right? But there's still something separating our hands. You still
can't feel everything, right?"

"You're right. I can tell you're using both hands, and I can tell you're holding my hand even though you're not moving. But it's like my hand is a little numb."

Hope removed the wrap and handed it back to Seshat. She took Skye's hand into her own, clasped it, and covered it with her other hand. Although Hope's hands looked tiny, Skye felt they enveloped hers. The skin felt baby soft, with no hint of callus, and the warmth astounded her. With her eyes still closed, she felt as if she could see the color in her touch.

"I can feel so much more now," Skye said, and covered Hope's top hand with her other hand. "I can tell how many fingers you have, feel your heartbeat." Her eyes flew open. "I can feel that you have *fingerprints*! I never thought about that!"

"Yes," Hope said. "That's what it felt like to me when you *saw* me and *heard* me and made me feel real, like that Velveteen Rabbit Daddy used to read to me about. I've never known anybody else who could do that. When your light turned all murky, I was afraid you might leave. And that scared *me*!

"But then I realized you need someone to see you and hear you too—the real you, the one you hide and protect. And I can do that for you, because you know I can't hurt you. If you stop now, in whatever way you're thinking about it, you'll never know the real you, the way I do. Can I tell you something I hear my daddy tell people sometimes?"

"Sure! Please do!"

"He quotes somebody named Robert Schuller, and he says, 'Anyone can count the seeds in an apple, but only God can count the number of apples in a seed.' You don't know how things will turn out until you see how things turn out.

"So, please, Skye. For me. For kids like me. For you. Come back downstairs, OK?"

"OK."

Silently, but with an almost physical SNAP, Seshat, Hope, and the endless white plain disappeared, and Skye found herself with her feet hanging over the edge of the parapet, her center of gravity forward, and flailing to catch herself.

A hand grasped the waistband of her scrubs so they cut into her abdomen as someone forcefully pulled her back. She scrambled off the parapet onto the roof, backpedaling, lost her balance and landed hard on her rear end.

Irene looked down at the hand she had used and said, "Damn! I broke a nail."

Skye looked stunned at first, then lay on her back and laughed out loud.

"I'm glad to see *your* mood has improved. I was worried sick when I couldn't find you!"

Skye sat up, propped on her hands. "So, what brought you up here? And, by the way, thank you!"

"I don't know. I just had a feeling. I think you might understand that." Irene smiled and sat on the parapet, took a deep breath, and slowly let it out. "She was here, wasn't she. Callie?"

"Callie, but in a different form. And I think she brought Hope up here, too. At least, Hope was here."

"Something happened while you were up here. Your vibe is on a whole different level."

Skye picked herself up, dusted the roof grit off her pants. She cocked her head a moment, smiled, and said, "I don't hear them anymore. The voices have gone quiet." She suddenly looked concerned. "Did something happen to them?"

"I doubt something happened to *all* of them all at once. I think it's more likely that you have learned how to tune your attention."

Skye scratched her temple. "How do you mean?"

"It's like when you and I were talking in the café last week. There were people at the next table talking, people standing in line talking, a TV yammering to itself in the corner, espresso machines hissing and popping, all kinds of sounds going on around us. But you had no trouble shutting out those background sounds to focus on our conversation in the foreground. Even when there's no extra noise, the sound of the HVAC is constant, but you don't notice it unless you listen for it. Audiologists call in 'central auditory processing.'"

"So, what, I'm learning central psychic processing?"

Irene grinned. "Something like that. I'd probably tend more toward intuitive processing. But then I like to say 'reality challenged' when we all know I mean 'crazy.' How about we get out of this wind and see how things are going in the ICU? I'm afraid we left Erica to deal with a mess."

Skye took a deep breath. "Can we go to the café first? I really need some caffeine, whether or not Callie is there."

***

Skye looked around the café as they entered, trying not to be obvious, but Irene picked up on it.

"I don't feel Callie. Do you see her?"

"No. She's not here as far as I can tell."

"Just as well. We need to chat a bit before we go back upstairs."

Skye sat on the edge of a chair, biting her lip. Her new-felt confidence from the roof had evaporated. "I know those kids need me, but I really don't want to go up there. Can't I somehow help at a distance? After all, I could still hear them on the roof."

Irene pursed her lips. "Well, I can't say for sure. I know of people who can do that. But that's not why we need to go back up there. You may or may not help children at a distance, but for sure there are people working up there who need some closure. And I suspect there are some parents who need it as well. We can't just leave them hanging, any of them. I can't make you, of course, but knowing who you are, I think you know you need to go back there."

They ordered coffee, Irene's plain black and Skye with plenty of sugar and cream, and went to what had become their favorite table. After they settled and took some calming sips, Skye looked off to one side. "So, you know who I am?" She looked up at Irene and waited.

Irene took a deep breath, let it out. "I don't claim to know anyone completely. But I have a strong sense of your heart. I sense your fear, but I can tell it's a shell protecting a tender heart. And

I can tell how strong you are inside. I could be wrong, of course. But I will be surprised if you don't decide to go back up there."

"But I have no idea what to do."

"You have no idea *right now*. I'm not at all sure I understand inspiration or where it comes from or how Callie works, but I don't think she puts ideas in your head. I think she helps you pull the ideas out of yourself. So I have faith that when you *need* to know what to do, you *will* know what to do."

"You and Callie both talk about believing in myself. What does that even mean?"

"We don't have time to dig into it much—I really think we need to get upstairs. But let me put it this way quickly. If I asked you whether you believe in Santa Claus, what does that mean, believe in?"

"That's like, do I believe he's real? Do I believe he exists? Right?"

"Sounds about right. On the other hand, if I ask whether you believe in me, I'm not asking if you think I'm real or not, correct?"

Skye smiled. "We could head off into one of those esoteric discussions, I guess, but for the most part, I don't think I'm imagining you."

"And I appreciate that! So what would the question mean?"

Skye pondered, looking off to her right. "I suppose it's like, do I trust you? Does that sound right?"

"Spot on. I could ask if you believe in me, or believe in Callie, or believe in your parents. Right now, though, what I need to ask is: do you believe in you?"

"Honestly? I don't know."

Irene gently took her hand and leaned forward. "I understand. I suspect you are about to find out. Are you done with your coffee?"

Skye looked at the empty cup. "I guess I can't put it off, huh?"

Irene smiled, but said nothing. Skye sighed, and said, "OK, let's go."

"Hold on just a second. I need to jot something down."

Skye pulled her notebook from the backpack while Irene waited patiently. In it she wrote:

Do I believe in myself? Do I trust myself? ??? ???

Skye put the pen into its receptacle, closed the notebook with a snap, slipped it back into her backpack, and sat back in her chair. She sighed, then said, "OK. Let's go."

They rode the elevator to the fifth floor in silence. Irene entered the ICU first and checked in with Erica, who told her Sasha Tidewater had left the unit. "She was pretty upset," Erica said. "I think she wanted a quiet space and some coffee. I told her I thought the one in the family kitchen was still broken, but she wanted to check."

"What about Dr. Powell?"

"He's not happy. He's always been open to anything that might help a patient. In fact, he's the one who let us try acupuncture on asthma patients. But he doesn't want anyone jeopardizing the unit's reputation, and if word gets out we're using psychics, he's afraid of the impact. After all, we're a nonprofit, depending on the goodwill of the public."

"I understand. Do you think it might be best if we sent Skye home for the rest of the day? I know it's been harder on her than probably on anybody else, and it's been a hard day all the way around."

"I think so. When Mrs. Tidewater comes back, I'll talk with her, but in the meantime, it's probably best to keep Skye out of here."

When Skye heard the news, she practically cried with relief. "Your willingness to confront the situation mattered here," Irene said. "You're very brave, and I appreciate your determination. I'll square things with your supervisor. You just head on home and get some rest."

She wanted to head back to the comfort of her parents' house, the home where she grew up, but she didn't feel up to more talk with her mom right then. In the middle of the afternoon, the old house that hosted the Rat Hole sat quiet and empty, all its residents at work or in class, so Skye could retreat to her own space and unwind in complete silence.

She took a long, hot shower, then toweled off standing in front of the little dresser that served as the only other bit of furniture besides the bed. To one side, the unicorn seemed to regard her with amusement.

"What are you looking at?" she said as she wrapped the towel around her hair. "You think this is funny?" She picked it up, sat on the edge of the bed, and regarded the little sculpture, turning it over, feeling calmed by the play of light on it through the gap at the top of the window curtains.

"So, you glory in being a unicorn. Great. But didn't you ever just want to be a horse?"

She put it back on the dresser facing her, its horn pointing over her head and shining in the light, as if pointing the way.

Skye sighed. "OK, fine. I'll figure out how to be... whatever I am. But I'm not ready to glory it in yet. Give me time."

She ran her blow dryer over her hair enough to not dampen her pillow, lay down, and almost immediately fell into a dreamless sleep.

***

When Sasha saw Grace in her wheelchair sitting at the small table in the family kitchen, she almost backed out quietly. She just needed some peace and quiet, and maybe some coffee, after all the rigamarole with Irene and Skye. But Grace looked up from her sketching, smiled warmly, and said, "Hi! I think we're neighbors."

Sasha smiled back shyly, and said, "I think you're right. I've seen you and your husband going in and out next door today."

"Yes. Our daughter, Hope, has been here for three weeks today."

"Oh, I'm so sorry!"

Grace shrugged, went back to sketching as she talked. "I'm not blasé about it, but we're sort of used to it. Hope is a 'frequent flier' here. They take good care of her. I'm Grace, by the way."

"Nice to meet you, Grace. I'm Sasha. This is all new to me."

"I remember our first time up here. It's a lot to take in. You came in late last night, right? Sit down, if you would like."

Sasha took the chair across the table. "Yes, we spent a few hours in the ER before they brought us up. It has been a real whirlwind!"

"How are things today?"

"Lakisha is stable, at least, though things are still touchy. I can't believe something like this could come from just petting some sheep!"

"Really! Wow! If you don't mind me asking, what's going on with her?"

Sasha explained about the school field trip to the sheep farm, the E. Coli infection, and the ER visit. "They say she's going to have to be on dialysis for weeks, maybe. And she's not out of the woods yet. Things could get worse!"

Grace nodded. "I can't imagine that particular scenario, but we've had several times when we thought we were losing Hope, no pun intended. She's always rallied, and my husband, with his weird sense of humor, always says, 'We haven't lost Hope.' I just roll my eyes."

Sasha laughed, and said, "Aren't they all like that? I think they crack dad jokes just to hide how much they feel something. I'll bet he was scared, for real."

"I don't doubt it at all. The folks here, not just the medical folks, but the social workers and the chaplains, they've always provided so much support, it really helps."

Sasha rubbed the back of her neck, hesitated. "I'm not sure I'm feeling that."

"What do you mean?"

"Well... I don't know. There was just some sketchy stuff going on this morning."

Grace put her charcoal pencil down and focused on Sasha. "What happened?"

"That social worker lady, Irene, she brought in some young girl that worked for housekeeping, not even a nurse or anything, and tried to get me to believe that gal could talk with Lakisha, hear what she was saying, even though 'Kisha is unconscious. I don't know what they were trying to pull, but I am not buying what they're selling."

Grace smiled and nodded. "I know what you mean. I had the same reaction at first."

"They been in trying that crap with your daughter too?"

"That was what I thought at first. I don't understand exactly how it works, but I had to change my mind—that young girl saved my daughter's life."

"Saved her life?"

"That's right. Oh, I couldn't believe it at first. But Hope had a pulmonary embolism going on, a blood clot in her lung, and because of where it was, it wasn't affecting her oxygen levels. But it was like a ticking time bomb in there. Since Hope can't talk, she couldn't tell us she hurt or anything, but Skye—that's her name, by the way—had already been, I guess you would say, talking with Hope. That's what my husband told me."

"You're sure about that? You're sure they're not just running some kind of scam on you?"

"I didn't know what was going on at first, just that Skye seemed to take an unusual interest in my daughter for someone who wasn't a doctor or a nurse. My husband told me he even asked her to stay away from Hope. But she got a message in the middle of the night from Hope, and she ran up here, risked her job in order to alert her night nurse. After my husband told me about it, I checked with her day nurse, who confirmed with the nurse who was on that night about what happened."

Sasha frowned, considering.

"I know it's hard to believe. I'm still trying to work it around in my head myself. But I can't think of any reason Skye would do that, risk her job and everything, unless she really wanted to help. I can't think of anything she would gain, and I can think of lots of things she could lose."

"Well, it's hard to see these scams coming. We had an awful experience with something like that before. My husband, Leonard, he got friendly with these people who were into using a Ouija board. Remember those? They seemed to just be playing at first, but one of them paired up with him and supposedly got a hot stock tip from his dead uncle, who had worked at a big oil company. Seemed to know things about Leonard that no one outside the family would know, that kind of thing. Long story short, they wound up talking him into investing our life savings into some bogus company stock, and then they took off with the money. Left us high and dry. We didn't see that coming! So I gotta wonder, what are they up to?"

"Have they asked you for anything?"

"Not yet, they haven't. I ran them out of there before they could work it."

Grace looked down at the sketch on the table for a moment, then looked up and said, "I can't tell you what to do, of course. We're all just trying to take care of our kids the best we can. And it wouldn't hurt to keep a close eye on things, certainly.

"But... she saved Hope's life, Sasha. I don't know what she might be able to do for your daughter, maybe nothing. But I know Irene has been at this hospital for 20 years. She's helped us multiple times, and there has been nothing the least sketchy about her. It's none of my business, but... you really might want to give what they're telling you another listen. After all these years of bringing Hope to the hospital, I've seen all kinds of things out of the ordinary. And my daughter may be named Hope, but I can tell you that when you have a child with challenges, you need all the hope you can get."

Sasha considered for a minute, biting her lip. "I'll think about it. Maybe I've been burned and think everything is on fire. But I'll think it over." She stood up. "That coffee machine is broken, is it?"

"I'm afraid so. Dan has been bringing coffee back from the little café over in the other tower. You can just walk across the bridge here and go down to the second floor. It will be right around the corner from the elevator." She leaned in. "By the way, you'll pass a little chapel on the way, if you'd like a place to just sit quietly for a while. I always find it a welcome respite."

"Thanks. I'll check out the coffee and the quiet. Lord knows I need both."

"Let me know how things go. We're probably going home to-morrow, but here's my email address." She scribbled on the back of a napkin and handed it to Sasha.

"I appreciate the encouragement, anyway. Good luck with your daughter!"

"And with yours!"

Sasha followed directions, intending to go straight to the café, but she saw the unobtrusive sign for the chapel and stopped. The peace inside almost immediately settled her down. The room had four rows of comfortable chairs separated by a center aisle, with kneelers on the front row. The wall behind the lectern featured a gorgeous stained glass depiction of a stylized nature scene, with dogwood blossoms and wildflowers in the foreground and mountains in the background. She looked closer, and could see, almost hidden by the artist, mini-scenes of butterflies, mice sleeping in a burrow, and grasshoppers playing fiddles and banjos. The whimsy made her smile. In the corner, a heavy oak cabinet fronted with glass panels displayed sacred objects from Christianity, Islam, Judaism, Buddhism, Sikhism, and Native American spirituality. On a wooden stand close to the entrance, a Bible lay open to Psalm 23, and a book next to it contained the scribbled prayers of parents and friends for the children in the hospital.

Sasha sat down in the front row. She didn't use a kneeler—that wasn't part of her tradition. But she prayed out loud.

"Lord," she said. "I don't know what to do. My little girl has been brought low, and we're in this strange place. I want to do what's best for her, but I'm scared, and I can't think straight. These people seem good, but those rats that stole our money seemed good, too. That broke Leonard, Lord, and that makes it hard to trust people. I can't do this on my own. I've always thought that fortune tellers and such went against your will, like when King Saul talked to that witch. But maybe you use all kinds of people to help all kinds of people. I'm just confused, Lord. If it's possible, I sure would appreciate some kind of direction, some kind of sign."

She heard something behind her, looked over her shoulder at the door, now slightly ajar, and recognized Erica.

"Oh, sorry! I didn't mean to intrude!"

"You're fine, honey. Come on in. This isn't my private space, is it? I reckon it's just a welcoming space."

Erica smiled. "Very much so. There's usually no one in here at this time of day, so I find it a good place to come sit quietly for a few minutes."

"It is that. Are you a believer?"

"Not so much in the conventional sense, I guess. I think there is something 'out there' bigger than my little self, and I'm open to whatever it is. I wasn't raised religious, but I've seen so many amazing things in my work here... well, it's hard to explain, isn't it?"

"I guess it is at that. I'll bet you've seen a miracle or three."

"Well, I've certainly seen things I can't explain. And I believe I've seen God working through the hearts and hands of the people who serve the children here—even through my hands, and, I've come to realize, through my heart. I think that may be as important to me as a nurse as my technical skills—but I wouldn't want to do without those skills! Still, they're not enough by themselves."

They sat quietly for a few minutes, then Sasha asked, "What led you to want to be a nurse in a children's ICU, anyway? I would think it would be a stressful profession."

"Oh, it certainly can be! But it can also be highly satisfying." She turned more toward Sasha and looked up, remembering. "I actually had a chance to move into a very high-paying position at a pharmaceuticals company. It would have meant not only a higher salary, but regular hours, and not having to stand on my feet all day. Painful feet just go along with the profession. My 'civilian' friends all talk about picking out pretty shoes, fashionable shoes, but my friends here swap tips about where to find shoes that stay comfortable and provide support for 12 hours."

"So, why didn't you take that?"

"I was going to. I had even put in my notice. But then I worked with a little boy who nearly died, and I was part of the team that helped him pull through. His parents sent me pictures of his eighth-grade graduation, and his high school graduation, and he even invited me to his wedding! The day he went home from the hospital, I asked them to tear up my resignation, and they did. I don't make as much money here as I could even at an adult hospital, but I couldn't get any greater satisfaction anywhere else. So I'm staying here as long as they'll have me."

Sasha considered for a long moment. "Can I tell you what I'm wrestling with? It's sort of the reason I'm in here."

"Please!"

"I guess it's not news to you that all that stuff with your friend this morning shook me up."

Erica looked crestfallen. "I know! And I feel so bad about it! We were just trying to help, but..."

"What you don't know is we, that is, my family has been scammed by people claiming some special abilities. I'm kinda touchy about things like that. And I felt like you, all y'all, were trying to take advantage of me. But I ran into a lady whose daughter has been in and out of here a lot, and not only did she sing y'all's praises all over the place, but she said that young girl specifically had helped her daughter, saved her life."

"That is true. I know who you're talking about. Of course, I can't say anything about an individual case, but I have seen that Skye has some way of connecting with people who shouldn't have any way of communicating. I don't know how it works, but it works."

"I'm still nervous. But... I can't see any way, now that I've calmed down, that she or you could gain anything out of faking this. So... if it was your daughter, would you let Skye try to talk to her?"

"Well, realistically, I've never had kids, so I can only speculate."

Sasha gave a small smile. "Oddly, that reassures me. If you were trying to put one over on me, you'd be building up how you've raised ten kids, trying to relate to me mother to mother."

Erica chuckled. "I think I satisfy all my mothering instincts right here in this hospital, but at the end of the shift, I can go home. I can't imagine what it's like caring for another human twenty-four seven, and I have a lot of respect for those of you who do. No, I can't directly relate. But I can tell you I've known Irene for a long time. She's another one who could have made a lot more money doing something else. But she's dedicated to the well-being of the children here, and their families. She also does free counseling for employees, even though it wasn't originally part of her job description. She's just a helper. So, if she believes in Skye, I believe in Skye. It helps that everything I've experienced with Skye just reinforces that belief."

Sasha took a deep breath. "OK. I'm going to go get some coffee, but when I come back, do you think you could get that young lady back in to try to talk with Lakisha again?"

Erica hesitated. "She's not here right now. She was so upset by things this morning that she went home early. But I'll see about bringing her in tomorrow morning."

Chapter Seven

Everything Changes... Again

S kye stood uncertainly in the doorway of room 510.

"Thank you for letting me talk with Lakisha again, Mrs. Tidewater. Erica said it was OK. Am I right in that?"

"I'm still not completely comfortable with it, child, but I'm willing to give it another go. I'm sorry I got upset with you yesterday. I've just had an awful experience with people claiming to know stuff they don't really know."

"I don't blame you. Honestly, it's hard for *me* to understand, but if I can help, I'm willing to try."

"Well, come on in. I'm hoping you can convince me and help 'Kisha."

Erica stuck her head in. "Everything OK?"

"I think so," Skye said, and Sasha nodded. "Do you have time to hang around? I'm not hearing Lakisha right now, but if I can talk with her, I may need some help. I don't know the medical stuff going on, and maybe I can let you check in with her and I can tell you what she says."

"OK, sure. I don't think I've ever assessed that way before, but I can learn something new."

Skye went to Lakisha's bedside and stood still for a while. Sasha watched closely. After a silent period Skye looked at Sasha. "Is it OK if I hold her hand?" Sasha nodded. Skye took the eight-year-old girl's hand in her own, remembering the feel of Hope's hands in hers. She closed her eyes. After a long minute, she opened them again, eyebrows knit. "I'm not hearing anything, not seeing anything. Maybe she doesn't want to talk to me."

"You haven't said anything, either," Erica said. "Maybe you need to start the conversation."

Skye gave a sideways grin. "Maybe you're right! I guess that would be the polite thing to do." She turned to the prone figure and said, "Hello, Lakisha. I hope I'm not disturbing you, but I'd like to talk with you this morning if you're OK with that."

Sasha saw Skye's gaze go from her daughter's face up to a point above her waist, and heard Skye say, "Oh! That makes sense. I'm sorry to interrupt."

"What's going on?" Sasha asked.

"Lakisha said she was playing with Hope in a dream, and I woke her up. But Hope is still asleep, so we can talk."

Skye turned her attention back to Lakisha, aware she could see what others in the room couldn't. "Lakisha, remember that your mom and Erica can hear only me, but I'll pass any messages on to them you give me. OK?"

"OK," astral Lakisha said. "Hope told me how things work, so I understand a little more about what's going on. Can you tell Erica that, ummm, I think she might want to get a little help to change me?"

"Oh! OK. I'll pass that on, and we'll give you some privacy." She turned to Erica. "'Kisha says she needs a change, and you might want to get some help. I'll step out."

"I'll let you know when you can come in again," Erica said.

"No need. 'Kisha will let me know."

Skye exited the room, astral Lakisha following, trailing a gossamer umbilical cord behind. Skye looked at her quizzically. "I don't really want to be there for this, if I can help it," Lakisha said, grinning as she floated along. "It's kind of nice to be able to be out of the room."

"That is kind of handy. Lots of times I wish I could be gone, like at the dentist, for instance."

"Am I going to remember any of this?"

"Honestly, I don't know. I was unconscious for a week or two when I was in the hospital when I was a little older than you, and I remember nothing from that. One day I was playing softball and suddenly I woke up in the hospital, with no sense of time having passed, even though two weeks had passed. Maybe I was awake on some level and poking around like you are now."

A couple of parents walking past looked at Skye, then one of them stage whispered to the other, "Earbuds change everything. In my day, if I had been standing somewhere talking to myself, people would have thought I was crazy."

"I know, right?"

Skye and Lakisha both heard, looked at each other, and burst out laughing. The couple looked back at Skye, who said, "Sorry!" and held up her cell phone. They smiled and moved on.

"I have a question, Skye. Hope told me what that silvery-looking string was called, but I can't remember. Do you know?"

"Callie told me it's called a *sutratma*. Does that sound like it?"

"I think so. Can you see mine?"

"If I concentrate, I can. Why?"

"Because mine looks a little fuzzy to me."

Skye squinted to better pick out the thin strand connecting Lakisha back to her body, passing through the closed door. She instantly saw that it looked frayed, with little strands of light splintering off and the whole cord thinner, appearing ready to break.

"Lakisha? Are you feeling OK? I mean, can you tell if there is something in your body that doesn't feel right?"

The door opened, and Erica gestured to another nurse. "Would you get Dr. Powell? We're noticing some erratic heart activity in here."

Skye's throat clenched. "Do we need to get back in there?"

"I think you probably should stay out here for the moment. We're going to have some extra folks in here."

Dr. Powell and another nurse ran past and closed the door behind them.

"What's going on? I feel funny," Lakisha said.

"I don't know, honey. But the doctor and the nurses are taking care of you. Just hold on."

Skye heard the pulse-ox alarm go off. The call light flashed on over Lakisha's door. Within seconds, the PA system came to life. "Code Blue, 510! Code Blue, 510!"

"Clear the way!" two more nurses shouted at Skye, and she stepped back as they rushed past with a crash cart, slamming the door behind them. Lakisha looked frightened and floated toward the ceiling.

"Where are you going!" Skye grasped Lakisha's foot, surprised to see a glow around her own hands, and pulled the girl down. The sutratma billowed, whipping like a fly-fishing line, thinning out.

Erica opened the door, finding Skye apparently grasping air. "Is she out here with you?"

"I have hold of her right now. What do I do?"

"How the heck should I know? You're the psychic!"

Skye looked up at Lakisha. Her expression had gone from fear to serenity. She hung calmly near the ceiling like a mylar helium balloon losing buoyancy. She regarded the silver cord with detached interest, and that frightened Skye more than if Lakisha had struggled. The cord looked thinnest just before it went through the now open door. Skye reached for it and found she could grasp it as easily as she could hold Lakisha's ankle, so she grabbed it with both hands.

"What are you holding now, and why are your hands glowing?" Erica asked.

"I don't know. All I know is it's fraying, and we're losing Lakisha."

Skye then heard a voice—felt more than heard, not out loud, but a feeling in her mind. A sudden insight clearly formed: "Tie a knot."

"Quick, if a surgeon needed to tie a line with a knot in the middle without cutting it, is there a knot they would use?"

"I don't know if they actually use it, but there is a knot called a surgeon's loop."

"Show me how to tie it."

Erica looked left and right, spotted a spare oxygen line hanging on a tank rack, grabbed it, and quickly showed Skye how to form a bight in the line, then make an overhand knot with it, but pass the bight through twice before tightening. Skye made the same motions with the sutratma, keeping the fraying spot within the loop that resulted. She pulled it tight, and the apparent stress on the cord relaxed, the frayed part smoothing out.

Inside the room, she heard a steady beep-beep from the monitor and the pulse-ox alarm shut off. Through the open door, she could see the medical team take a step back, the doctor standing next to Lakisha's body holding defibrillator paddles ready to apply, stopped in mid-treatment.

"What just happened?" Dr. Powell said.

The sutratma cord dragged astral Lakisha in like reeling in a fish. Still looking calm, Lakisha waved, and the cord drew astral Lakisha back into physical Lakisha, where the young girl began to snore.

From her chair to the side, Sasha let loose the breath she had been holding. "Would somebody please give me a clue what just happened to my little girl?"

Dr. Powell pulled in a deep breath of his own, blew it out with a soft *whew*. "Well, Mrs. Tidewell, it's rare, but sometimes HUS can lead to cardiac complications such as myocarditis, heart failure, or arrhythmias. These complications could cause sudden cardiac arrest. That appears to be what happened to Lakisha."

"I don't know what half of that even means. Are you telling me my eight-year-old daughter had a *heart attack*?"

"Not exactly, but close. Her heart briefly stopped beating. But just as we were getting ready to try to restart it, it started up on its own."

Erica and Skye looked at each other, and Erica smiled. "Good job," she whispered.

"I need to go home," Skye said, shaking, looking ashen.

"Sit down for a few minutes first." Erica cradled Skye's elbow as she escorted her to the nurse's break room and brought her a steaming cup of tea from her own stash.

***

Before Skye could even assemble her cleaning cart for the day, her supervisor pulled her aside.

"HR wants to talk to you before work today, Skye," he said.

"What about?"

"Just go up there, now. They're expecting you."

Skye had only been upstairs once before when they had hired her. Even her training and orientation had taken place in basement rooms or conference rooms in one of the two towers. The administrative level above the original hospital hardly ever needed access by day-to-day employees. Skye took the dedicated elevator to it with trepidation.

"Come in, Ms. Jackson, and have a seat."

The small office screamed "institutional"—standard issue metal desk, beige walls, analog clock hung to the side. On the small desk sat two huge monitors. The imprint of filing cabinets still pressed into the thin carpet, but piles of paper sat on the desk around the monitors. *Looks like he's still getting used to computers,* she thought.

"I'm Tim Reynolds, Ms. Jackson, and we have asked you to come to HR today because we have heard that you may be interfering with the medical personnel."

Skye's throat tightened. "Interfering? I'm not sure what you mean."

"Well, it's not that you're getting in the way so much as that you may step outside your lane. Our Environmental Technicians have no business engaging in therapy, formal or informal, and we have had a report from a nursing supervisor that you have been, um, *helping* some patients in the ICU. You even got smack in the middle of a rapid response team reacting to a Code Blue. That's a problem in itself, but it's more for the medical staff to deal with.

"But from a job standpoint, we have a bigger problem."

What else could it be? Skye sat quietly, waiting for Reynolds to go on.

"Would you be interested in what that problem might be?"

"Yes, sure, I was just waiting for you to continue."

"Uh huh. Well, several times in the last three weeks you have left early, called in sick, neglected floor mopping, etc., because you have been so busy 'visiting' with patients—which is not your job. We understand you even went to the ICU after midnight one time, which was not even your floor at the time, and then missed half a day the next day, letting the cleaning duties pile up."

Reynolds cleared his throat. "I realize cleaning is not the most glamorous job in the world, but it's an important one in any setting, especially a hospital. Do you realize you are the first line of defense against the spread of infection?"

"Yes, absolutely, it's why..."

"And that if you Environmental Technicians don't do your job, the medical folks won't really be able to do their jobs?"

"I know, it's really important to..."

"So when you let your curiosity about patients impede doing your job, you actually endanger those patients. Do you understand that?"

"I would never want to..."

"You have been in a sort of probationary period, Ms. Jackson. You only hired on a little over a month ago, and I have to say that in a lot of ways, you didn't seem to know you were being scrutinized."

Reynolds propped his elbows on the desk, steepled his fingers, leaned forward, and looked intensely at Skye. "I have a daughter about your age, Ms. Jackson, and I think I understand some of what goes on with young women in college. She worked at Krogers and got fired because she assumed somehow the job belonged to her, that she had things nailed down, and she didn't really have to work all that hard. She spent too much time socializing with others in the break area, only halfway did her duties, and called in sick on a whim.

"I've seen that sort of thing in your generation far more than I care to. I hope that this experience will be one you look back on and see it as a turning point, that it helps you to develop a true work ethic. In any case, your services are no longer required at this hospital. We will pay you for the hours you have already put in today, such as they are. Please get your things out of your locker."

Skye sat stunned. After a pause, she said, "I'm fired?"

"Terminated."

"No warnings or anything? Three strikes? At least a heads-up?"

"You were on probation, Ms. Jackson. It didn't work out. That's all. I'm sure you'll find something else soon in this labor market, perhaps in fast food. We will mail your final check to you. Have a good day."

Numb, Skye collected her extra set of scrubs (*guess I won't need these after all*) and turned in her badge. "Can I go up to the floor and say goodbye to people?" she asked her supervisor.

"Not a chance. That's the sort of thing that got you fired. If you go up there, you're likely to have the security folks help you find the door."

Someone gave her a cardboard box that had once held gallons of industrial cleaner. She sat in her car in the employee's garage, the fragrance from the loaded box drifting up to her nose, and considered her next steps.

Soon, she would have to come up with tuition for next semester. Her rent would be due in eleven days. She wouldn't be on the street, thank God, since her parents would let her move back in. But...*my parents! What am I going to tell them?*

Exhaustion coupled with sheer overwhelm washed over her. She put her head on the steering wheel, sobbed softly for a minute, then fell into sleep.

***

Dan stood beside Hope's bed, softly stroking her hair. She slowly closed her eyes.

"I hope that means you're enjoying that," he said. She slowly opened them again, slowly closed them, then opened them again.

"We're getting ready to take you home. At least you'll be in your own bed again. I had hoped Skye could come by and see you before you headed home, but there's someone else on the floor today."

Hope gazed steadily ahead. Dan never knew if she actually saw him when she did that. He moved slightly to one side, and her gaze didn't shift, so he assumed she looked right past him.

"But I'm sure Skye will always remember you, and that she cares deeply about you."

She closed her eyes again, and it may have been Dan's imagination, but it seemed as if a slight, peaceful smile crossed her face.

His phone rang. Grace had pulled the wheelchair van around to the patient discharge door, so he could start hauling material downstairs before getting a nurse to help him move Hope.

He began loading bags and equipment onto the cart the hospital brought them, talking to Hope as he went.

"You know, I always wondered if you heard us when we talked to you. That's one of the things Skye taught us: always assume your kids hear you, even when it looks like they can't—or won't. I used to joke that you were just like any other teenager. You didn't listen, just for a different reason."

Dan paused in his packing and looked at Hope. "I'm sorry about that, by the way. I know now that you listened probably a lot better than most teenagers. And I also learned that the things you say when you think nobody is listening could be some of your most powerful words. I've often said you are my greatest teacher, and that's just one more thing you've taught me, with Skye's help."

He looked up at the ceiling, smiled, and dug out his red sketchbook. "In fact, I can use that in a book somewhere. I'm going to write that down before I forget it. But don't worry—I'll give you the credit."

He drew a quick picture of an ear, and underneath it wrote:

> The things you say when you think nobody is listening could be some of your most powerful words. ~Hope Roberts

He went back to loading equipment to take home: ventilator, bottles of saline flush, sterile water, suitcase of custom hospital gowns, overnight bag, extra oxygen tubes, overnight bag for himself, another for Grace, three or four stuffed animals. He made two trips to get all that down to the waiting van. Then he loaded Hope's necessary equipment onto her wheelchair: oxygen tank;

portable suction machine; portable pulse-oximeter; pink bag with spare clothes, diapers, wipes, GJ tube extensions, catheters, etc. He looked around and realized he almost forgot her "go bag" with its load of essentials: spare trach, ambu resuscitation bag, finger pulse-oximeter, copy of her current Medical Administration Record, copy of their conservatorship papers, and three or four heat and moisture exchangers for her trach.

"Moving you is like planning for D-Day," Dan said. "But we'll make sure all contingencies get covered."

He heard a soft knock at the door, turned to see Sasha peeking in, smiling. "Getting to go home?"

"Yes, finally! We're used to the coming and going, but it's always a challenge packing up all her stuff. How is Lakeisha doing?"

Sasha beamed. "She woke up this morning! She's still groggy, but she kept talking about her dreams and playing with the little girl next door. I'm still thinking about all that, but I can't tell you how glad I am that 'Kisha is on the mend. I wanted to thank your wife for her pep talk. Is she still here?"

"I'm afraid you missed her—she's down with the wheelchair van, waiting for us to bring Hope down. We're a two-wheelchair family. If we get another one, we'll have to get our own bus!"

"I'll bet! Please tell her I stopped by, will you?"

"I would be glad to. In fact...."

Dan opened a portfolio next to where Grace had sat and pulled out a piece of watercolor paper.

"Grace said I should give this to you if I saw you. She said she didn't know why she drew this, but she thought you might like to have it."

Smiling, Sasha took the paper, looked it over, and caught her breath, her eyes widening.

"When did she do this?" Sasha asked.

"Just a couple of days ago. In fact, I think it was right after she had a conversation with you. I guess that's why she thought of you. Knowing Grace, I'll bet she kept drawing while she talked, right?"

Sasha nodded. "She amazed me how she could draw and talk at the same time."

"That's my Grace. She's always drawing or crocheting or beading or something all the time, even when she's talking or watching TV or, I don't know, doing open heart surgery. I guess I'm biased, but... it's really good, isn't it?"

Sasha turned back to the paper in her hands, eyes wide, and slowly shook her head. "That's not the half of it. Y'all never met 'Kisha, did you?"

Dan looked thoughtful. "No, I don't think so. We didn't want to intrude on your privacy, and I don't think we've seen her heading for a procedure or anything."

"So neither of you has any way of knowing what she looks like, right?"

Puzzled, Dan said, "I guess not. Why do you ask?"

Sasha turned the paper around. "Because I've never seen a better portrait of Lakeisha. It even shows that little birthmark above her left temple. But this can't be Lakeisha right now. If I didn't know better, I'd say this is Lakeisha in 15, 20 years."

Dan took the paper, looked closer. "I'll take your word for it, but she's a fine young woman in this watercolor. I see she has a stethoscope around her neck." He squinted. "I can make out a name on the white coat. It says, 'Lakeisha Tidewell, MD.'"

He handed the paper back to Sasha, who gazed at it wordlessly for some time while Dan stood silently. She looked up with tears in her eyes. "I don't have words. Just tell Grace she's given me a vision."

"I will do that. Good luck with everything."

"It's all going to be OK. Thank you." She turned and quickly left the room, holding the paper close.

Dan smiled, shook his head. "Amazing Grace," he said to himself. "She just can't help but touch people."

He buzzed for the nurse.

"Can I help you?"

"Could you let Erica know we're ready to go?"

"I'll send her right in."

Ten minutes later, Erica came in, looking worried.

"Everything OK?"

"I'm not sure. I was going to bring Skye in to say goodbye, but someone else has the floor today."

"I noticed that."

"So I asked, and although they're being cagey about it, it turns out that Skye got fired this morning."

Dan froze. "Wow! I didn't see that coming. Why?"

"I'm not sure. I suspect word may have gotten to the wrong people that she had been sort of 'helping' the medical staff, and they probably got spooked."

He considered for a moment. "Do you have any way of getting in touch with her?"

"We never traded contact information. I'm not sure anyone here outside HR knows, and they won't release information like that. Privacy and everything."

Dan sat down, shook his head. "I really hate to hear that! Not only for Hope, but, selfishly, for me. I know for sure now that Hope can hear and understand what we're saying, but Skye provided the only way for her to talk to *us*."

Erica nodded, started to speak, hesitated, then plowed ahead. "May I share an observation with you, Mr. Roberts?"

He smiled. "You know, I think that's the first time someone has called me by name. It's usually just 'Dad.'"

"I know. That happens all over the hospital. We have soooo many parents to keep track of, it just makes it easier. But thanks to Hope and to Skye, I feel like I've gotten to know y'all a little better than most."

"Then call me 'Dan.' I'm more likely to know who you're talking to. 'Mr. Roberts' just confuses me."

Erica smiled back. "Thank you. I was just thinking about Skye and everything that went down here the last three weeks or so. I know she has been a big help. You may or may not know that these last three weeks were also the first that she even knew she could talk with children like Hope."

"I hadn't really thought about it. I guess I thought she'd always done this sort of thing."

"She was starting a new job, too, and I don't know much about her home life, but I know she had some challenging circumstances—money for school, rent, all the usual stuff facing young adults these days. And, yes, she's an adult, but she's a *young* adult, not even able to legally drink yet. I'm certain she's only 19 or 20."

Dan looked over at Hope lying passively in the hospital bed. "That's the same age as Hope. But Skye seems so much older!"

"Well, I think we would all agree that Hope is special. And as I've come to know Skye, I'd say she is an old soul. Still, as helpful as she's been, I think all of this, and I mean *all* of this, has been hard on her. That was *before* she got fired. I understand that you have lost something significant. But she's already done far more than expected of her, and she has given y'all an incomparable gift. Maybe it's just time for her to, you know, move on. Not just from the hospital, if you know what I mean."

Dan nodded wearily. "I appreciate both your tact and your candor. Life with Hope takes constant readjustments, and from my perspective, this is just one more. But you're right. I'm very grateful for what Skye has done for us, and I only wish her the best."

He reached into his shirt pocket and pulled out a business card. "If you hear from her, would you share this contact information with her? For that matter, if there's ever anything I can do for you, I would happily do so. Your care for our daughter has been fantastic. I appreciate everything you and the other nurses and doctors and therapists and technicians and cleaning staff and ... well, everybody *here* has done for her and for us. You are everyday heroes. Thank you."

Hope's pulse-ox monitor briefly sped up, then settled back into a steady rhythm. Dan smiled again. "I think that may be her way of saying, 'Amen.'"

"And so it is. Now, let's get Hope settled in her van to head home."

***

Skye fell through clouds, not plummeting, but drifting down slowly, as if dropping through wads of cotton. Her hair fluttered slowly around her as she dropped, with no fear of falling but clearly not flying, almost as if in a weak gravity field.

The clouds opened up, and she could see the land coming toward her in slow motion. She wondered if she would wake up when she hit the ground, whether it would hurt, whether she might die in real life. The air around her spoke and said, "You're dreaming, Skye. You might even be dreaming you're dreaming. No worries, no one dies."

Below her, she saw a small rectangle that got bigger and bigger. She realized she fell toward it, and soon it resolved into a bed, piloted by Hope, who expertly maneuvered to bring Skye to a soft landing on its backend.

"Are you sleeping on the job?" Hope said, continuing to steer with both hands as they swooped toward the ground.

"I don't have a job anymore. So, no, I'm not sleeping on the job, just sleeping."

"Oh! What happened?"

"They fired me. They said I wasn't cleaning good enough, and I guess I wasn't, but I really think they didn't quite know what to do with me."

"That sucks! You were one of their best assets."

"Guess they didn't think so. If I'm seeing you here, you must be sleeping too."

"I'm actually on my way home, sleeping in the wheelchair van. Like Daddy always says, when the going gets tough, the tough go to sleep. Anyway, I wondered why you didn't come see me before I left."

"They called me in first thing this morning, and then after they fired me, they wouldn't let me come upstairs. I'm sorry."

"Me too. I had hoped you might pass on a message or two. Mom and Dad have always believed I could hear them and understand, and now they know for certain, but they still can't hear me. Hang on!"

Hope pulled back on both reins, sending the bed into a roller coaster loop while shouting, "Wheeeeeee!" Skye gripped onto the side railings, though she didn't feel likely to fall off.

"Do you think you could come see me at home?"

Even in dream state, Skye felt her chest tighten, and a tear ran down her cheek. "I don't know, sweetie. Your parents would have to invite me, and they don't know how to get in touch with me.

You can't tell them, either—if you could, you wouldn't need me. I don't see how we could make that happen."

Hope brought the bed to a perfect landing in a clearing in a forest. On one side of the forest, an outdoor kitchen featured five people madly whipping up various recipes, and in the middle stood a woman shouting, "Thirty minutes left, people!"

"What's all this?" Skye asked.

"I'm just playing back one of my favorite episodes of 'Kitchen Delight.' It's one of those food competition shows."

"So you don't eat, but you like to watch food shows?"

Hope shrugged. "I guess it's like lonely people who read romance novels. I have no idea what that stuff tastes like, but it looks good, and I like to watch people cooking. What can I tell you?

"Anyway, about that 'need you' thing. You really helped me, and I hate the hospital was stupid enough to fire you, because you could have helped a lot of other kids. But just because you don't work at the hospital doesn't mean you can't help kids. Plus, I didn't ask you to come see me because I *need* you. I want you to come see me because you're my friend."

In her car, still leaning on the wheel, tears escaped from Skye's closed eyes, reflecting what she felt in dreamworld.

"I'm glad," Skye said, "and you're my friend, too. I've never had a friend like you, and I'm glad I do now."

The bed dissolved, depositing them gently on the ground, and they walked toward the frantically working cooks.

"We can always visit in the dream world," Hope said. "The thing is, though, it seems like not many people remember their dreams.

Since 'Kisha woke up, I'm not sure she remembers me. I run across people in my dreams a lot of times. Some of them I know, and they never say anything to me about what we did in dreamworld. There's even one of my nurses I see regularly in dreamworld, but when she comes to work, she never says anything about it. It's just not the same as being able to, you know, *talk* with you."

"Who knows, maybe something will work out? This is still all so new to me. I have no idea how things are going to go."

Hope reached into the pockets of her dress and pulled out a handful of butterflies. She released them into the air, where they spiraled around her and then swirled up to disappear high above them. "Did you know Daddy says I'm his greatest teacher?"

"I have not heard that, but I'll bet it's true. What have you taught him?"

"He says that nobody knows what's going to happen, how things are going to turn out, but people *think* they know how things will go. They think their kids will go to school and go to college and get married and have a career and have kids and make all this money and bring them grandkids, but life has a way of throwing curve balls. I think that has something to do with baseball.

"Anyway, he says I've taught him to make your plans, but hold them lightly, because they're going to change. He says they have the *illusion* of predictability. He always says it like that. Like 'ih LOOOOOOO shun.' And he says the only difference between him and Mom and everybody else is that he and Mom have been literally DIS-illusioned. They *know* that you never really know what's going to happen, with your kids or with anything else. And you just have to live your life anyway, one step at a time."

Skye pondered that. "You know, I think your dad is right. You are a pretty great teacher."

"Thanks. I think you're pretty good yourself."

"Oh, yeah? What could I teach?"

"You could teach people it's important to connect. And to listen. I mean really *listen*. To each other, but also to your *heart*."

"That sounds a lot like Callie."

"She's a pretty good teacher, too. Well, the van has stopped, and that means they'll be hauling me inside soon. I don't know when I'll see you again, or if you'll remember when I do. But I want to thank you for being my friend. And I hope..."

A rapping on her car window jerked Skye out of sleep. A hospital security guard looked in on her. "Are you OK, Miss?"

She rolled down her window. "Sorry, yes, I'm fine! I guess I didn't get enough sleep last night."

He looked at the wet spots on the steering wheel from her tears, noted drying rivulets on her cheeks, but said nothing about it. "Happens all the time here. You gonna be OK driving home?"

"I just need to get some coffee, I guess."

"Looks like you have some right there, still hot. Enjoy!"

He pointed to the fresh, steaming coffee in a brass insulated mug in her center console and smiled.

Skye followed his finger and saw a sticky note attached to the mug's handle. She picked it up and read, in most elegant handwriting, "Enjoy! Callie." She looked at the guard as she picked up the mug and smiled. "I will," she said. And then a little more softly, almost under her breath, "I sure will."

***

Skye looked over potential classes for spring semester for the fifth time, even though it looked as if she wouldn't have the money to pay for them, and she really didn't want to ask her parents to help. It sucked bad enough that she would probably have to move back in with them, since the rent came due in less than a week. Besides, she had missed so many classes the last few weeks around the drama at the hospital that she felt certain she would have to repeat the courses from fall semester. It would put her behind, but she couldn't think of an alternative.

She sipped the tea from the brass mug Callie had left her. Whether she made tea or coffee, the mug kept it at exactly the right temperature, no matter how long she let it linger. Any other time in her life, it would have amazed her. After her recent experiences, though, it seemed almost mundane.

She closed her laptop, deciding to figure out the class thing after she figured out the money thing. Just then, her phone lit up. She didn't recognize the number, so she let it go to voicemail. Minutes later, a text came through from the same number. "Hi, this is Irene. I just tried to call you from my personal cell. Would you please call me at your convenience?"

Irene? Why would she be calling me? Maybe she just found out they fired me.

She hesitated, but curiosity ultimately led her to call.

"Skye, thank you for calling me back! I have something I wanted to run by you."

"You know I don't work there anymore, right, Irene? I'm sorry I didn't let you know, but I got fired last Thursday."

"Yes, I know. When you didn't show up for your appointment, I called the ICU to check on you, and Erica told me what happened. I am so sorry to hear that! I thought I had worked things out with your supervisor, but someone further up the food chain had other ideas. It's sort of why I'm calling."

"Isn't it a little unusual for a social worker to do an exit interview? I would think HR would do that, although they didn't seem interested in doing anything except getting me out of there as fast as possible."

"I'm not calling on behalf of the hospital. I'm calling for *me*."

"OoooKay. I'm not sure I understand."

"Let me put it this way. I've been thinking for some time that maybe it was time to move on to the next phase of my life. I've definitely been fulfilled working with the people at Foothills Children, but lately not so much. Nothing wrong with them. I just feel constrained by the institutional limits."

"Yeah, I know a little bit about those limits."

Irene chuckled, but continued. "I've known for some time that I could take early retirement, and I had been considering it more seriously lately. After what happened with you, a little voice told me that now is the time. Who knows, maybe it was Callie! Anyway, I have tendered my resignation from the hospital, and I have put down a deposit on a new office. I'm opening a private counseling practice."

"Wow! Congratulations, I guess. That sounds like a big step!"

"It is. And it's one you helped me realize I needed to make. And that brings me to the reason for my call.

"I'm going to need help around the office. That involves some things like answering the phone and helping make appointments. But my practice won't exactly be conventional. I don't just want an office manager. I want a true assistant. Maybe even something like an apprentice. And I can't think of anyone who would fit better than Skye Jackson. Would you consider taking this job?"

Skye held her breath for a second. Irene took it as hesitation and said, "If it makes any difference to you, you might like to know that I already have some clients lined up. One of them is someone you know, and I think you would be key in helping them with their needs."

Skye's heart quickened. "You wouldn't be talking about...."

"Because of patient privacy laws, I can't say right now. I just think you would make a tremendous difference. For whatever it's worth, just as I was considering calling you, they called *me*, wondering how to get in touch with you. The hospital would only tell them you no longer worked there.

"It won't happen quickly. We have some 'set up' to do first. Let's just say that her parents truly have hope for this situation."

Deep inside she felt/heard something saying, "What are you waiting for?"

"Yes. Yes. Yes! Oh my God, yes! When can I start?"

"Got any plans this afternoon? I could sure use some help figuring out this computer."

"Hey, I'm just a medium, not a miracle worker. But I'll see what I can do."

Skye heard Irene muffle a laugh. "Sweetie, the proper term is 'psychic.' A medium helps communicate with those on the other side—dead people. But if you can figure out this computer, you may save its life. Otherwise, the computer will *need* a medium."

***

Skye gathered up her things to go meet Irene before they drove together to the Roberts's home, humming happily to herself in anticipation. Even though Irene had set up the visit last week, she still rode the high that came following that phone call. It seemed destined, almost, that Irene would run into Dan and Grace at a Trader Joe's when neither of them shopped there very often. Irene said the first thing Dan asked was whether she had contact with Skye, and it thrilled them to hear that Irene had succeeded in bringing her into private practice.

"They are working on transitioning Hope into the adult care system, and they would like our help to navigate that," Irene had told her. Since Dan's insurance listed Irene as a counselor, it would even cover their services—officially, for family counseling. But they had tons of questions about the system change, and mainly, they hoped to not only leverage Skye's abilities, but also Irene's intuitive understanding of the challenges they faced.

In fact, Irene quoted Dan as saying, "Any help you can provide in figuring out the ridiculous state bureaucracy is a serious benefit and bonus. But the real benefit comes from being able to learn what Hope wants for herself during this period of her life."

While Skye brushed her teeth, she thought about how things had changed in the last year. She now had a good-paying job, flexible enough to work around her class schedule. She also had a fantastic mentor in Irene—one who understood how to bring out her best. True, she had lost a semester and had to retake classes to erase the impact on her GPA, but her new major in Social Work gave her a new sense of direction.

Even the little things improved her life. For instance, she no longer had to keep her microwave in the bathroom. Having her own little kitchenette, even if it was part of a studio, gave her more satisfaction than she would have predicted. Plus, she had room for a couch and a couple of chairs to invite friends over—so much better than the old Rat Hole.

For that matter, she now had friends. They even knew her peculiar history, and they still hung out with her!

As she left the bathroom, she noticed the iridescent notebook on her dresser beside the unicorn statue. She always carried the notebook with her, occasionally jotting notes to herself, exploring ideas, mind-mapping, even making grocery lists. When insights of inspiration struck her, she preserved them there. Despite its rough treatment riding around in her backpack, it showed no signs of wear and tear, its colors as bright and shifting as ever, the wires of its spiral perfectly round, its corners sharp. The black pen in its receptacle never ran out of ink.

Why is it out on the dresser? she thought. *I'm sure I haven't touched it in a few days.*

She picked it up to replace it in her backpack, taking a moment to appreciate its weight and texture, enjoying its warmth. That's when she noticed the bookmark in it, one she didn't remember placing.

She opened the notebook to the bookmark and found three pages that had somehow inserted themselves immediately after the last note she had written in the hospital café, the one in which she had asked herself if she trusted herself. The paper fit perfectly but looked different from the rest of the pages, resembling the yellowed pages she found in old books in the university library. The pages held a message written in elegant, flowing script that looked familiar, in ink that seemed to float above the page.

Dear Skye,

It has been such a pleasure seeing you grow into your full measure. I know your journey isn't finished. As long as you are on earth, it won't be. But you have achieved something most people struggle with their whole lives. You have figured out who you are.

It doesn't take intervention from anyone outside of yourself to do that. After all, it is what humans were made to do. Siddhartha Gautama, the historic Buddha, once said, "Your purpose in life is to find your purpose and give your whole heart and soul to it." You are doing that, and in so doing, you foster connection everywhere you go. You may find that your special ability to hear and see those who cannot communicate with others on this plane of existence may fade with time, but your special creativity will always lie in fostering connections.

You, of course, have a special ability. What may not be obvious is that many, many people walk around every day, seemingly visible to everyone, and yet unseen and unheard. They hide their true selves, presenting a mask to the world, or they play small so that others look right at them but do not see them. Loneliness is an epidemic in the age in which you live, and you are a cure for that.

There is a character that people think is fictitious, but they have a basis in ultimate reality, the reality that goes beyond the mundane. They have said, "Everyone is a story in the end. Make it a good one.[2]" You are telling your own story, and you are helping others to tell theirs. You go now to help someone you have helped before, and you are, indeed, a lifeline for young Hope. You are also a lifeline for her parents—not only in connecting them to her, but to each other more strongly, and each of them to their purpose and creativity.

You have not been aware of my presence in the last year, but I have been with you. I do not experience time the same way you do, and that same character I mentioned before has taught me an excellent lesson: no spoilers. But I didn't want to just disappear out of your life. And so I leave you this note of encouragement. In some ways, I may have inspired you, but all I did was to help you pull your real self out. You did the work. I only midwifed, and what you have brought forth inspires me, and inspires the world, whether or not the world knows it.

Another wise man named Howard Thurman said, "Don't ask yourself what the world needs. Ask yourself what makes you come alive, and go do that, because what the world needs is people who have come alive." You have truly come to life, and you have helped and will continue to help others to do so as well. It was a true honor to work with you, to help fulfill my own purpose. As your Muse, I may have inspired you. But you also inspired me. Thank you.

P.S. Tell Dan I said hello.

It was signed "Calliope, a.k.a. Seshat."

Skye closed the notebook and held it to her chest, eyes closed, and smiled. "I've known you were there all along, Callie," she said. "I don't have to see you or hear you to know you're with me, that you *are* me, maybe the best part of me. I don't know if you hear me and see me the way I used to hear and see you, but it's still important for me to say: thank you. Thank you for everything. Thank you for what you and your sisters do for humanity. And thank you for helping me to be a part of that."

She opened her eyes and said to no one in particular. "All righty, then. I think it's time to go facilitate some connections."

Lessons Learned

There are lots of notes in *Medium Well*. Skye wrote some down. Dan wrote others. Yet others appeared in various places. To help you consider the insights they represent, we have gathered them all here.

- Writing is a great thinking tool. Ironically, it helps you master detail *and* see the big picture.

- Write it down yourself. That will make it your own.

- Sometimes talking with someone else helps you hear yourself more clearly.

- Your belief in yourself is more important than whether someone else believes you.

- Listen to yourself. Listen to your heart.

- What looks like an accident could be the start of something wonderful.

- Fear can blind you. Look again.

- There's believing. And there's believing *in*.

- A unicorn doesn't try to be different. It simply is what it is.

- The things you say when you think nobody is listening could be some of your most powerful words.

"Dreams are illustrations from the book your soul is writing about you." — Marsha Norman in her 1987 novel *The Fortune Teller*

Discussion Guide

M any readers may want to explore *Medium Well: The Journey from Believing to Believing In* together in their book clubs, business study groups, houses of worship and community groups, or among friends and family. The questions below may help in guide your discussions.

1. What challenges might you be facing now or have faced early in your career?

2. Skye finds herself looking at the world and seeing something different from what everyone else sees. When you have had a different point of view, how did it make you feel?

3. Have you ever been in a situation where nobody seemed to hear you? How much difference did it make if and when someone connected with you?

4. Have you ever been the connector for someone?

5. When you doubt yourself, what are some steps you can take to get a realistic view?

6. Who is someone who has acted as a mentor to you?

7. Do you feel comfortable seeking professional counseling, or do you assume anyone who needs such "must be crazy"?

8. How do you react when someone questions your motives? Have you experienced both sides of that situation?

9. What does it mean to believe in yourself? What do you need in order to do that?

10. In what way do you have a genius or a muse? How does it feel to recognize that?

11. Have you ever taken a chance to help someone in need, or have you played it safe? How did you feel afterward?

12. What does the unicorn mean to you?

13. Have your intentions ever been misconstrued? Have you ever misread someone else's intentions?

14. Which is better, to be overly trusting or overly suspicious?

15. Have you ever been fired? How did you react? How did you recover?

16. Think about a time when something bad happened that turned out to be something good. How did that unfold?

17. Take a look at "Lessons Learned." Which of the insights from the narrative mean the most to you?

Author's Notes

I've had several discussions with fellow business parable authors like Jeff West and Bob Burg. We agree that an effective business parable must involve at least two overarching factors: it must tell a good story apart from the lessons taught, and it must offer life-building lessons in some fashion. You may have read parables lacking in one (or, sadly, both) of those. I hope both the story and the lessons in *Medium Well* serve you with engaging entertainment and useful insights. If not, these notes will do little good. If so, you may have some curiosity about certain elements, and I hope to honor that here.

Where did the story originate?

If you read the previous book, *The Way of the Three-Year-Old Why*, you already knew Dan Roberts and his daughter, as well as Callie. (If you're not familiar with that book, you can learn more at DonnKing.com/3yo.) Whether Muses are "real" (see the section below), human experience certainly supports the sense of their reality, and my muse kept nudging me to continue their story. In fact, I had planned for another book to come second in the

Sparklight Chronicles. I intend, still, to write and publish that book (the first chapter of *Real Speak* comes at the end of this book), but the story of Skye and Hope suddenly thrust themselves to the front of the stage.

Medium Well started when my daughter, Hannah, went into the ICU at East Tennessee Children's Hospital in September 2023. Like Hope, Hannah has a very rare chromosomal disorder. Hannah has been hospitalized somewhere between 35 and 40 times in her life (we have lost count), but this was the first time she was admitted straight to the ICU from the ER, and the first time that she spent the entire time (three weeks) there, discharging straight to home.

ETCH is an amazing institution, staffed by people on a mission. Erica, in particular, represents a cross-section of many nurses with whom we interacted. For the curious, we did not have someone like Skye who would spend time with Hannah, but we noted the dedication with which the housecleaning staff approached their jobs. They, too, are on a mission, though I don't know how much appreciation they receive for it.

I posted a real-life observation about "Insights from the ICU." (You can read it at DonnKing.com/ICU.) Parents deal with decisions no one should ever have to make. Staff deal with the impact of high-intensity, high-pressure work. I wanted to write a story about that.

At about the same time, I heard a podcast from author and speaker Mel Robbins in which she interviewed an intuitive psychic who had appeared on her show before. (If you're curious, you can watch the interview at DonnKing.com/MelPsych.) As Kim Russo talked with Mel about her experience serving as a channel for connecting people on different planes of existence, I thought how wonderful it would be if someone could provide a link like that with people like my daughter.

We get clear indications that Hannah can hear and understand what goes on around her. She just has no volitional control of her body in any way that allows her to communicate back. It's not a coma. It resembles "locked-in syndrome." It tears at my heart sometimes. I wish I could give her some means of communicating back to us.

I work with people to help foster communication, so the parallel for a business parable seemed obvious.

It turned out I actually knew someone who could shed light on the experience of providing such a conduit. I talked with Michaela McGivern (MichaelaMcGivern.com), who not only advised me on how such things work, but also visited with us and acted as a channel for us with Hannah.

If you're curious, Michaela inspired the character of Irene more than she did Skye.

From there, the story evolved in classic "what if" storytelling fashion. With NaNoWriMo (NaNoWriMo.org) coming up, it seemed the perfect opportunity.

Do you believe in psychic mediums?

To tell you the truth, I'm not sure. Here's what I know. I know I could see Hannah responding to Michaela, relaxing and engaging in the extremely limited way that we have seen from her over the years. Hannah has never had the ability to even give stereotypical "blink once for yes, twice for no" responses. But we have been able to, with patience, get some indication of what she wanted with a simple "blink for yes." (I made use of that in an interaction facilitated by Skye in the story. The description of how we used "blink for yes" there fits how we interact with Hannah, minus the intervention of someone like Skye.)

I know Michaela believes in her abilities, and I believe those abilities are real in terms of helping people. I *know* she does not take advantage of people. I *know* she helps people.

Do I understand how it works? Nope. But I don't know how my microwave works, either.

But aren't you a pastor? How can you support this [fill in the blank]? How can you posit the actual existence of Greek deities?

There are several answers to this.

1) It's fiction, at least that part. In no way am I suggesting the realities of psychic abilities (though I am open to the possibility) nor of Greek demigods (which are, at best, allegorical or psychological). But they sure make for good stories. In fact, there's quite a lot of evidence that even in ancient times, most people under-

stood mythical explanations as attempts to understand that which cannot be understood rather than records of factual happenings.

To make the point somewhat controversially, few readers, if any, ever seemed to have a problem with J.R.R. Tolkien writing about elves, dwarves, wizards, and hobbits. Nor do many (if any) complain about C.S. Lewis featuring a talking lion and a magical portal into a parallel universe, even though they were Christians—maybe *because* they were known as Christians.

Tolkien never leaves his mythical universe, though Lewis grounds at least some of his stories in what would otherwise be a "normal" recognizable household. If my use of demigods disturbs anyone, it may be because so much of the world I describe is recognizable as the same as ours. Although a business parable incorporates elements of both fiction and nonfiction, if this book were strictly fiction, it would probably fit a genre known as "magical realism."

In other words, it's just a story.

In modern times, we equate myths and legends with "untruths" or even "lies," as in "urban legends." However, throughout most of human history, storytellers simply didn't care about such distinctions. Truth went deeper than mere factuality. "Did this really happen?" was an almost useless question. Story is how humans have made sense of their experiences as long as we have been human. More important than "Did this really happen?" is "What does this mean for me?" So...

2) Don't get hung up in the story. A parable is not meant as a textbook explanation of anything. It is a vehicle to carry some

deeper truths forward. To give a (I hope) noncontroversial example, very few people get hung up on whether the Parable of the Sower or the Parable of the Weeds in Matthew 13 involved real incidents. Readers, whether Christian or non-Christian, understand Jesus intended to impart a lesson, not give a report.

The story of Skye and Hope teaches nothing about Greek deities or psychic phenomena. It deals with doubt and uncertainty, learning to trust yourself, the importance of communication, and the difference between believing facts and believing *in* people.

3) Having said that, I would also like to make a point about the supposed division between spiritual beliefs and science. You may or may not have an interest in such things, and if you do, I would encourage you to download the bonus chapter for this book. You can get it at DonnKing.com/MWBonus. Readers will have noticed that part of Skye's dilemma involves a perceived contradiction between her growing abilities and her religion, and she considers having a talk with Pastor Tim. The bonus chapter records not only that conversation, but a key insight that helps Skye on her personal journey.

The short version: just because we don't understand it doesn't mean it's not scientific.

One more question: what's in the note that Callie sent Grace?

I wish I knew. I think I may have to write another book to find out.

Bottom line

I hope you found the story of Skye Jackson, Hope Roberts, and
Callie both enjoyable and inspiring.

Acknowledgements

Writing is a solitary profession, but it also takes a village. Many people have affected *Medium Well* in direct and indirect ways. Among many others, I would like to acknowledge and thank the following.

Alexandra Russell, acupuncturist, for her insights into the energetic body.

Dr. Corky Harrison, RIP, professor in Speech and Theatre at Murray State University. You taught me that reality behaves as if it is out there.

Shell Vera, whose editing greatly improved this story in every way. Her eagle eye and passionate heart offered a uniquely valuable skill set and encouragement.

Michaela McGivern, who provided insights into the process by which most psychic mediums operate, as well as into medical practice based on her years in a hospital setting. Note: I have, at times, used the term "medium" where actual practitioners would use the term "psychic." That was for stylistic reasons, but I want to acknowledge that Michaela made sure I knew the actual difference.

In other words, it isn't her slip-up, but my obstinacy. She was the perfect teacher.

The Go-Giver Success Alliance, a wonderful community of people dedicated to living by principles reflected in this book, whose support helped give it birth.

Joanna Penn, whose example and mentorship have been a guiding light for many years. Without her, none of The Sparklight Chronicles would exist.

This book is dedicated to the health professionals who keep our daughter alive, but I must mention them in the acknowledgements as well. I am amazed at the home health nurses, the hospital nurses, the ICU nurses, the doctors, the physician assistants, the nurse practitioners, the phlebotomists, the lab technicians, the ER doctors and nurses, the imaging technicians, the pharmacists, the records-keepers, the admissions specialists, the insurance sherpas, the social workers, the environmental technicians, the food service people, the volunteers, the chaplains, the wound-care specialists, the carpenters, the security guards, the social workers, the building engineers, the telephone operators, the billing specialists, the marketing professionals, the fund-raisers, all the folks at East Tennessee Children's Hospital who somehow bring it all together for children like Hannah. May your sense of mission carry you through the most difficult times.

First chapter of Real Speak

Here's a little background on the next book in The Sparklight Chronicles. It's an open secret that *Real Speak* was
supposed to be the second book in the series. In fact, I got about a
third of the way done with it when Skye Jackson and Irene Duguid
showed up along with Callie and Hope and insisted on jumping
the line. In fact, the first printing of *The Way of the Three-Year-Old
Why* had the first chapter of *Real Speak* at the end instead of the
first chapter of *Medium Well: The Journey from Believing to Believing In*.

Therefore, if you happen to have a print copy of *The Way of the
Three-Year-Old Why*, the following may look familiar. (If you have
an ebook, it likely updated to include the first chapter of *Medium
Well* instead, in which case this may all be new.)

Real Speak focuses on Harold Wilson and Sam Jennings, two
different people facing real-world challenges in their careers. Callie
shows up along with another of her sisters, and a new antago-
nist seeks to scuttle their work along with Harold's and Sam's

careers. Dan Roberts cameos in a small but important role. Along with reading a good story, readers will learn more solid principles for effective communication in the third book of The Sparklight Chronicles.

You might like to know that just as I was wrapping up *Medium Well*, my Muse came calling once again, and blessed me with the structure for a fourth book. The working title, adapted from conversations with my editor, Shell Vera, is *Hurting Hands, Healing Hearts*. I can't say a lot about it right now, but I can tell you it will focus on Grace Roberts and a significant development with Hope Roberts, in a good story with life principles on dealing with grief, crushed expectations, and healing. Stay in touch.

***

One thing Harold knew for sure. Visualizing them naked didn't work. In fact, it had the opposite effect—trying to do so just made *him* feel naked.

Still, he knew he had done his homework, that he knew all the facts he needed to present, and that he had plenty of data on his slide deck to back himself up. He also knew that if he had any hope of moving up in the organization, he had to get past the memories and at least tolerate speaking to the other supervisors.

I've got this, he thought to himself. *They're always telling you to think positive. So I'm thinking positive. I've got this.*

He took a deep breath, picked up the clicker, and launched into it.

"How's everyone doing today?" he said.

Sam Jennings, sitting in the front row, sighed almost imperceptibly and sneaked a look at her watch. Some of the others stirred, and a couple mumbled things like, "Fine." "Good." "OK."

"Well, let's get right into it, then. I have a lot of information to share with you, and I know I'm standing between you and lunch. You'll notice from this chart that in the third quarter our project revenue was good, but it was down about 4 percent compared to the same period a year ago...."

***

This could have been an email, Sam thought. She had already seen Harold's written report. *Why do I have to waste time sitting through yet another boring meeting?*

Sam doodled on her legal pad, hoping it looked as if she were taking notes. Sitting on the front row had probably been a mistake, but he wanted to be visible to the C Suite folks. She had seen Elizabeth Martinez quietly slip into the back row, and she knew if she wanted to move up, she had to been seen as a leader.

Sam certainly wanted to move up. She knew the C's talked a lot about leadership, and she understood the term, at least in a dictionary sort of way. She just couldn't quite wrap her engineer's brain around such a fuzzy concept.

Materials specifications, she understood. Spreadsheets made sense. Math worked the same every time. But people? People made less sense than silly putty.

As Harold droned on about the division's earning, Sam's mind wandered back to a conversation with Martinez at the end of last year.

"No one can top you for tech knowledge, Sam, and you're the best when it comes to troubleshooting projects," she said. "I really want to bring you up into higher leadership, but there's a bit of a problem. We've had this conversation before, and since I come from an engineering background and I also relate to the challenges of being a woman in a highly male-dominated field, I think I can understand why those conversations haven't led to the hoped-for outcome."

Sam had listened intently, disappointed but determined to solve this problem the way she solved geometric dimensioning and tolerancing equations or figured out a new feature on the CAD software.

"Because of that, I know you probably don't want to hear this, just like I once didn't want to hear it," Martinez continued. "And just like I needed to hear it clearly, without ambiguity, I'm going to tell you plainly: you will advance no further, in this company or almost any other, unless you gain some measure of 'people skills.'"

"You mean like the marketing folks use? That's just so much sleazy, fuzzy fluff!"

"One of the first thing you have to learn about it is that sleazy doesn't cut it. And although you can't count it the way our accounting folks count dollars or our design folk measure failure rates, it is far from fluff. Solid, scientific studies support the impact of of effective communication strategies."

Sam scoffed. "Scientific studies? If you're talking about focus groups and so-called 'qualitative studies,' I would hardly call them scientific."

"Call it what you will. The results can be replicated. The fact that you're arguing with it shows the basic problem. Again, I'll state it plainly: getting over that kind of attitude was the linchpin that changed my career. Do you have any idea how rare it is for an engineer to become a VP of Sales for any major corporation? Fewer than 10 percent. Want to guess how many of those are female?

We're out there, but we're almost unicorns. You don't have to pursue that C-Suite office. There are others. But until you understand sales and marketing, you have no hope of getting beyond your current level.

"And sales and marketing means you have to understand people. By the way, if you understood even the basics of dealing with people, you probably wouldn't disparage the marketing folks when you're talking to the marketing person most in a position to help you."

Sam looked shocked and began to stammer, "Oh! I'm sorry! I didn't mean to.... I mean, it didn't, um, I meant, ah.... Really, I'm sorry, I wasn't thinking."

"Yes, you were. You were thinking. You were thinking exactly the way you have always thought—like an engineer. That's not a bad thing at all. I don't want you to stop thinking like an engineer. It's not a matter of either-or. It's both-and.

"Here's the thing, Sam. As an engineer, you have an advantage for the C-Suite. You know how to analyze problems and determine criteria for the solution. You know how to gather and analyze data. You can take complex ideas and break them down into logical components. All of that is necessary for success in any 'Chief' position. It's just not sufficient, not without the people skills. Why do you think you have so much turnover in your section?"

"I think we keep hiring people who can't handle the feedback they need to hear."

"We're losing good people, Sam, and our competitors are hiring a lot of them after they leave us. They manage to thrive at other companies, a lot of them. Do you think those companies just don't give them the feedback they need?

"No, I'm sorry, Sam. You can't blame the people. We're hiring the best raw talent out there, and they need a leader. A leader. Not a manager. A leader. That's going to take people skills."

Martinez stood up, and so did Sam. "We've hired a consultant. You're not the only supervisor having this problem, so we want her to work with several of you. But, Sam, you have to take her seriously. And I mean, seriously. We don't just hire talented designers. We hire talented designers with potential. That's why you're here. You have the potential to truly lead.

"But potential doesn't always pan out. That's why we're bringing in a consultant name Ama Terasu. You may not have heard of her, but she's the one who guided me when I was in your shoes. I know you have a supervisor's meeting to attend, so I'll let you go. When she calls you this afternoon, do us both a favor: take her call, and make sure you pay attention to what she tells you. Deal?"

Sam swallowed hard, but she looked back at Martinez steadily and said, "Deal. Thank you for believing in me."

Martinez looked grim. "Justify it. I know you can. I'm waiting to see if you will."

"Anyone have any questions?" Harold said.

Sam snapped back to the present. She looked around quickly, saw Martinez in the back row looking straight at her. She studied her legal pad, now covered with geometric figures and quadratic equations, as if seeking a note. Harold looked around hopefully as silence held. People began to squirm and check cell phones. After a long silence, Harold said, "Well, I guess that means we covered everything. No questions? All right, good, well, um, everyone have a good rest of your day."

Sam's phone buzzed. She checked the text and saw that it was from A. Terasu. "Good time to chat?" the text said. *Guess I'd better get to the office. I really don't want anyone else hearing this conversation.*

***

The time flew by for Harold, and he barely had a memory of what he had said and done. But he knew he had covered all the material, and he had kept it under an hour. In fact, he had sped through the material in only 40 minutes, which he figured would be a relief to the other supervisors. After all, Harold knew how many meetings he himself had sat through hoping that they would soon be over.

As he carried his laptop down the hall toward his cubicle, Harold nearly crashed into Elizabeth Martinez coming out of the break room.

"Whoa!" he said as he tried not to knock her coffee cup from her hand. *It's probably not a good idea to cream your Vice President,* he thought, but he said, "I'm really sorry! I should have been watching more closely. My apologies!"

She had looked startled, but Martinez recovered quickly. She always seemed to maintain her cool no matter what happened, a trait Harold sought to emulate with varying success.

"No harm, no foul," she said. "I'll bet you were thinking about the presentation you just gave."

"Were you there?"

"You bet. That project is an important one."

It was Harold's turn to look startled. He had not noticed Martinez, but it probably was a good thing he had not. His nervousness would have gone up like a fourth of July rocket. Still, it turned out to be an opportunity. He knew he had given a clear picture of just exactly what the project challenges were.

"Do you mind if I ask you what you thought? I'm open to feedback."

Martinez looked at him for a thoughtful moment, then said, "Are you sure?"

"I'm sorry?"

"Are you sure you're open to feedback? Let's be honest. Most people to really want feedback. They just want to be told what a good job they did."

Harold swallowed, but plowed ahead. "I would appreciate any genuine observations you can make. I think."

"Why?"

Stuttering just a little, Harold replied, "I really want to move up in the company. I need to have an accurate idea of how I'm doing if I am going to do that, and I can't think of a better person to give me that, if you're willing, than my VP. So give me the bad news. I can handle it."

She chuckled. "Don't assume it's bad news. But it probably deserves more than a hallway conversation. How about this? There's a Toastmasters club that I know about that meets on Wednesday mornings at the coffee house a couple of blocks over. Why don't you check them out tomorrow morning, and meet with them for two or three weeks. Maybe even join. Then you can tell me how you think you did. You can even watch the recording."

"Recording?"

"Sure. You didn't know we were recording the presentation? As I said, it's an important project."

The thought of listening to himself talk filled Harold with dread, but he didn't think that was a smart revelation to the boss. He just said, "That's great! It certainly gives me an opportunity for growth."

Or humiliation. Maybe it will just prove I'm not promotable.

"Perfect," she said. "See you in the morning, then. I'll email you the address."

She'll be there too? What have I gotten myself into?

About the Author

D onn is an associate professor of communication studies at Pellissippi State Community College in Knoxville, Tennessee, and a pastor in the United Methodist Church, as well as a speaker, writer, and communication coach.

He works with professionals and leaders who want to speak confidently so they can increase their impact, gain influence, and build their careers.

He has spoken to audiences, churches, and radio audiences across the United States and written numerous newspaper, magazine, and blog articles. He authored *The Right-brained Guide to Parliamentary Procedure: A Path Through the Forest* and co-authored *Responsibly Spoken*, a textbook on public speaking. He wrote *The Way of the Three-Year-Old Why*, the first book in the Sparklight Chronicles, followed by *Medium Well*.

Donn is a proud member of The Go-Giver Community and The Go-Giver Success Alliance with Bob Burg and Kathy Tagenel. He has been a guest on podcasts and shows such as *Write Your Book in a Flash* hosted by Dan Janal, *Business Inspiration* hosted by Dana Morgan Barnes, The *Be Better Broadcast* hosted by Brandon Eastman, and *The Nashville Association of Sales Professionals* hosted by Terry Lancaster.

For over 40 years, Donn has taught college students and business leaders the skills of effective communication. In recent years, he has guided dozens of professional speakers, teachers, and presenters in the effective use of Zoom for engaging communication. He is the winner of the Excellence Award and the Innovation Award, both from the National Institute for Staff and Organizational Development.

He has earned a B.A. in communications from Freed-Hardeman University in Henderson, Tennessee, and an M.S. in communications from the University of Tennessee, Knoxville.

Donn is married to Janet. Together they have five children, four of whom survive, three of whom are grown and independent, and one of whom is... complicated. Donn and Janet live on the quiet side of the Great Smoky Mountains, where Donn teaches and writes, and Janet makes amazing creations from yarn, and where they enjoy the best coffee in Tennessee.

Also by Donn King

- *The Right-brained Guide to Parliamentary Procedure: A Path Through the Forest*

- *How Our Health Care System Got Sick, and How to Cure It (If We Dare)*

- *Responsibly Spoken: A Manual for Public Speaking and Business and Professional Speaking*

In the Sparklight Chronicles series:

- *The Way of the Three-Year-Old Why: Live What Really Matters*

- *Medium Well: The Journey from Believing to Believing In*

- *Real Speak* (planned for late 2024)

1. . Easter egg for fans. If you don't get the reference, we're nodding to Doctor Who. For background, look at https://en.wikipedia.org/wiki/Doctor_Who

2. . Another nod to Doctor Who.